THE MASSEY LECTURES SERIES

The Massey Lectures are co-sponsored by CBC Radio, House of Anansi Press, and Massey College in the University of Toronto. The series was created in honour of the Right Honourable Vincent Massey, former Governor General of Canada, and was inaugurated in 1961 to provide a forum on radio where major contemporary thinkers could address important issues of our time.

This book comprises the 2022 CBC Massey Lectures, "Laughing with the Trickster," broadcast in November 2022 as part of CBC Radio's *Ideas* series. The producer of the series was Philip Coulter; the executive producer was Greg Kelly.

TOMSON HIGHWAY

Tomson Highway is a Cree author, playwright, and musician. His memoir, *Permanent Astonishment*, won the 2021 Hilary Weston Writers' Trust Prize for Nonfiction. He also wrote the plays *The Rez Sisters* and *Dry Lips Oughta Move to Kapuskasing*, and the bestselling novel *Kiss of the Fur Queen*. He is a member of the Barren Lands First Nation and lives in Gatineau, Quebec.

T0275500

LAUGHING WITH THE TRICKSTER

·····························

On Sex, Death, and Accordions

TOMSON HIGHWAY

ANANSI

Published in Canada and the USA in 2022 by House of Anansi Press Inc.
www.houseofanansi.com

House of Anansi Press is committed to protecting our natural environment.
This book is made of material from well-managed FSC®-certified forests,
recycled materials, and other controlled sources.

House of Anansi Press is a Global Certified Accessible™ (GCA by Benetech)
publisher. The ebook version of this book meets stringent accessibility
standards and is available to readers with print disabilities.

26 25 24 23 22   1 2 3 4 5

Library and Archives Canada Cataloguing in Publication

Title: Laughing with the Trickster : on sex, death, and accordions / Tomson
Highway.
Names: Highway, Tomson, 1951–author.
Series: CBC Massey lectures.
Description: Series statement: The CBC Massey lectures
Identifiers: Canadiana (print) 20220206961 | Canadiana (ebook) 20220207011 |
ISBN 9781487011239 (softcover) | ISBN 9781487011246 (EPUB)
Subjects: LCSH: Tricksters. | LCSH: Wit and humor. | LCSH: Mythology.
Classification: LCC GR524 .H54 2022 | DDC 398/.45—dc23

Series design: Bill Douglas
Cover design: Jennifer Lum
Text design: Ingrid Paulson
Typesetting: Lucia Kim

*House of Anansi Press is grateful for the privilege to work on and create from
the Traditional Territory of many Nations, including the Anishinabeg,
the Wendat, and the Haudenosaunee, as well as the Treaty Lands of
the Mississaugas of the Credit.*

 Canada Council
for the Arts
 Conseil des Arts
du Canada
ONTARIO ARTS COUNCIL
CONSEIL DES ARTS DE L'ONTARIO
an Ontario government agency
un organisme du gouvernement de l'Ontario

With the participation of the Government of Canada
Avec la participation du gouvernement du Canada |  Canadä

*We acknowledge for their financial support of our publishing program the Canada
Council for the Arts, the Ontario Arts Council, and the Government of Canada.*

Printed and bound in Canada

MIX
Paper from
responsible sources
FSC
www.fsc.org   FSC® C103567

"The straight line is godless and immoral."
— Friedensreich Hundertwasser,
Austrian artist and visionary

"The Power of the World always works in circles."
— Black Elk, Oglala Lakota medicine man

CONTENTS

ONE

On Language

TAANSI, NIWEE-CHEEWAA-GANAK, TAANSI. (Hello, my friends, hello.)

Nihee-thiwee-win, eeya-goo neetha n'ta-yamoo-win. (Cree, that is my language.) Eeya-goo aya-moowin n'gaa-pachee-taan oota masin-a-eega-neek. (That is the language I will be using in this book.)

How, kaachi-moostaa-tinaa-wow igwa. Ootee waathow keeweet-nook neetha kaagee-neetaa-weegi-yaan. Kwayas kayaas eeya-g'waani-ma kaa-i-tamaan. Maw peeyak iskool igootee kee-ayow. Mawch igoo-speek. Igoochi keespin nigee-weeskoo-loowin, poogoo tasi-p'weetee-aan. Poogoo tana-gata-wag'wow ninoo-taawee-gaanak. Poogoo tana-gata-maan n'taski. Igwaani igoosi

n'geetoo-teen. N'gee-sipwee-taan igoospeek
keegach teepagoop poogoo kaagee-tawtaw-
skeewin-eeyaan. Sawa-nook ni'gee-tootaan.
Kwayas waathow sawa-nook. Oopaas-kooyaak
keesi-theegaa-tao anima ooteenow itee kaageen-tay
tagoo-sinee-yaan. Igoota kaagee-skooloo-wiyaan.
Keegaam-taa-aat aski igootee kaagee-ayaa-aan.
Maa-a taatoo-neepin nigee-geewaan tantay-
weecha-a-mag'wow neet'saa-nak. Neepin, ispeek
maawachi kaami-thathaw-stik saagay-higan igwa
maawa-chi kaamaa-mithoo-geesigaak. (Now,
I will tell you a story. I was born in the Far North.
That was a long time ago. There was no school up
there. Not back then. That's why, if I wanted to go
to school, I had to leave home. I had to leave my
parents. I had to leave my land. So that's what I did.
I left when I was almost seven. I went south. I went
very far south. The Pas was the name of the town
where I went to school. I lived there for nine years,
though I went home for two months every summer to be with family: July and August, the best
part of the year, when the ten thousand lakes that
are our home are at their calmest, the days at their
longest, the weather at its most balmy.)

Cree is a northern language, at least for
Canadians who live right next to the U.S. border,

which is most. So far north does the language live that most have never heard it, much less speak it. However, for the Dene (pronounced "Day-nay") and the Inuit — that is, for the peoples whose ancestral lands are the vast territories of Yukon, Northwest, and Nunavut — Cree is southern, so far south that it might as well live on the beaches of Rio de Janeiro. Cree, that is to say, lives between the two extremes of north and south, as Canadian a concept as one can get. We speak here of the northern half of our country's six largest provinces. A good third of the nation, one would like to say, if not for the fact that Nunavut alone is the same size as all of Western Europe.

In the early decades of the twentieth century, five young Cree adventurers from North Central Saskatchewan started making inroads into Canada's subarctic. They rowed boats made of timber that were built for transporting trade goods northward and furs back south for a British fur-trading enterprise called the Hudson's Bay Company. Navigating an incredibly complex and incredibly rich drainage system of lakes and rivers, they fell in love with what they saw, a land spectacular beyond all expectation. And they stayed. My dad, Joe Highway, then just a lad of eighteen years, was one of them.

The fact that Cree-speaking Metis and half-breeds started trickling into this area throughout this same period provoked the decision. The original definition of the term "Metis" was a person who was half Cree and half French, as the French root of the term, "moitié," means "half." French fur traders, after all, were the very first Moony-ass (our name for Europeans, a charming word like "folks" or "buddies") to arrive up there, thus passing on to us such family names as Dumas, Michele, and Merasty. A half-breed was a person who was half Cree and half English, Scottish, Irish, or even Orcadian — someone from Scotland's Orkney Islands — all strains of Moony-ass who arrived up there after the French. The term, however, is outdated; almost insulting, it is no longer used. To attest to such Anglo or part-Anglo ancestry, Cree families in Northern Manitoba today still bear such names as Cook (my mother's maiden name), McKay, and Flett, the last still the most common name on the Orkney Islands. That the women of marriageable age in this burgeoning community were fetching was no deterrent either. Refugees from a historic rebellion in Southern Manitoba named after its leader, Louis Riel, my mother's forebears formed part of this northward migration. My father decamped from

Northern Saskatchewan to Northern Manitoba to wed my mother and stayed so that we, too — like the Ojibway and the Mohawks of Ontario and the Blackfoot of Southern Alberta — straddle a border, if only one that is provincial and not international.

This was how the Cree language arrived in the northwest corner of Manitoba, one prong from the southwest (Saskatchewan) and one from the southeast (Manitoba), on land that was situated so far north that it was no longer Cree territory but Dene. And thus it was that within one generation of uneasy coexistence between these peoples — Dene, Cree, and Cree-speaking Metis — many among them became bilingual. In Cree and Dene (but not French or English). My father was one. And it was only a matter of time before those aforementioned Cree adventurers and their progeny, my father among them — though this time with a wife and the first two of what would be a final tally of one dozen children — penetrated even farther north, thus encountering the true Arctic people: the Inuit. And learned their language. At least, my dad did. Which is how, when you add to the mix the pidgin English he had managed to absorb in his youthful dealings with the Hudson's Bay Company as a rower of York boats, those vessels that transported furs in relays from northwestern Manitoba to Hudson's Bay, my father, Joe Highway, came to speak four languages: Cree, Dene, Inuktitut — the language of the Inuit — and English, not one of which comes from the same linguistic family and so are as different one from the other as English is from southern Slovakian. In a country filled with people armed with doctorates in English literature, business administration, and quantum physics, and who speak but one language, Joe Highway, a man who never set foot in a single school for a single day, Cree caribou hunter and legendary world championship dogsled racer, spoke four.

Like all northern men of the time, my father had this way of leaving his wife and toddlers at home in the shelter of a cabin at our home base of Brochet (pronounced "Bro-shay"), a village of some eight hundred souls located some two hundred kilometres south of Nunavut, and wandering the vastness of the low subarctic and Arctic by himself for days, even weeks, at a stretch. It was the lifestyle — they were hunters; tracking game was their bread and butter. Dad used to say that on windless days — keeping in mind that the nearest human being lived ten thousand kilometres north of where he stood — he could hear the earth breathe. Her lungs — bogs, swamps — rising and falling and rising and falling like a giant human heart. And humming, one extended note as pure as sound can be.

With no one else to talk to, he talked to his sled dogs. "Cha" for "right," "U" ("you") for "left," and "Marches" for "forward." Borrowed from the French verb in the single imperative, "marches," pronounced like the English "marsh" and meaning "walk," is a command that was later adjusted by anglophone dogsledders to the simpler though more prosaic "mush." The language was basic, but the animals got it. The lead dog, in particular, who was picked from the litter and trained for the role from birth, would lead her teammates left, right, and forward, according to the call of the driver at the helm: my dad, Joe Highway. (Because of the smell of a certain organ found only on females, lead dogs were always female; thus, they have their "penitents," their ardent followers.)

Our Elders like to say that there was a time eons ago when humans and animals spoke one language, so Dad would summon moose with a honk, loons with their signature haunting ululations and mating calls of grunts combined with gurgles, beavers with a hiss, and owls with a hoot. It was only a matter of time before these sounds morphed into verbs and nouns: "moosaw" for "moose," "mawg'wa" for "loon," "amisk" for "beaver," and "oo-hoo" for owl. A shepherd in ancient Greece would have done the same on the rock-pocked slopes of his sun-splashed Arcadia, cooing at his sheep, clicking his tongue to guide their movements. Some linguists say this is how human language was born. Having heard such verbal exchanges myself, I believe it. As with the story of creation — of the universe, the planet, humankind — no one really knows. And because no one knows, theories proliferate. One theory is that language comes from gestures transmitted from one animal to another and, later, from one human to another. Another is that it come from sounds — cries, for instance, wails, barks — likewise transmitted. Communication between mothers and newborns is another theory. Evolution, progress, grammatical development for the purpose of sur-vival — they all factor in.

Poets, artists, and shamans would have taken over to give personae to these forces of nature and these landscapes. And from such potent ingredients would have risen the divine beings that now popu-late the planet from one end to the other. Or at least did at one point in the past. Yes, indeed, languages do come from acts of magic, of all-out wizardry, of shamanism. They come from that universe of miracle unending called world mythology.

So if the world is filled with languages, then it so follows that the world is filled with mythologies. Why? Because it is languages that not only gave birth to those mythologies but also gave them the form and the character they have today. The question being: What does the term "mythology" mean? Where does it come from? As most European languages are based, to a greater or a lesser degree, on the language of the ancient Greeks and their successors, the ancient Romans, it comes to us from the Greek words "mythos," for "narrative," and "logos," for "word" or "discourse." Put together, the hybrid word thus means "a word" or "a discourse" on "narrative." Mythology's closest cousins, which are so close that they can be easily confused by the unvigilant, are theology, which comes from "theos" ("god") and the aforementioned "logos," and cosmology, where "cosmos" has been variously defined as "world" or "universe."

The difference between these three "discourses"? Theology is a discourse on gods only. Cosmology is a discourse on the universe only. And mythology is a discourse on both gods and the universe. Gods on one level, humankind on another. This

is a writing technique I learned from such dispa-
rate artists as William Shakespeare, particularly
in his play *A Midsummer Night's Dream*, where
humans cavort with fairies; William Butler Yeats
in his hearkening back to figures from Celtic mythology such as Cuchulain, ancient Ireland's equivalent
of ancient Greece's Hercules; and Canada's James
Reaney in his treatment of the very human members
of the Donnelly family as, at one point, constel-
lations and, at another, archetypal figures from
Christian mythology. That's the kind of narrative
that concerns me in my work. And that's the kind of
narrative that concerns us in this book.

Over the years have I come to believe that,
through the course of much human movement
across this planet, three mythologies in particular have come to a meeting point, a kind of forum,
here on our North American continent. And not
only have they come to exchange information at
this forum, they have changed to accommodate one
another in some way, in the interests of mutual sur-
vival. They have mixed and mingled and emerged
as a hybrid. And it is this hybrid of three mythologies, as I see it, that has had the most to do with
giving form and substance to North American
thought, life, and culture as we know it today.

The first mythology is Christian. The second is Christianity's immediate predecessor, ancient Roman, which emerged from ancient Greek, the two constituting another hybrid, one scholars call classical mythology. And the third? North American Indigenous mythology. There isn't, strictly speaking, just one such mythology — Canada alone has more than one hundred Indigenous languages and therefore one hundred mythologies — but there is enough similarity between them for us to call them another hybrid here, for simplicity's sake.

We can understand Christian mythology because we speak English and French and any number of other languages, mostly European, that articulate this mythology, if in translation from the original Hebrew or, in the case of the New Testament, Greek. The same goes for the mythology of the ancient Greeks and Romans, because we have access to literature, if again in translation only, that expresses it. Works by Greece's Homer and Plato and Rome's Virgil are the least of it. But the same rule does not apply to the Indigenous languages of Canada, mostly because they were, until recently, unwritten. Most Canadians do not even know that more than one hundred Native languages once existed in this land, and although

several have died, many are still very much alive.
Most Canadians have never heard the Cree language in conversation. Most don't even know
that many words in everyday usage — such as
Saskatoon, Saskatchewan, Winnipeg, Manitoba,
Chicoutimi, Quebec, and Ottawa — are Cree. And
if they do, they don't know their meaning.

Yes, indeed, the word "Quebec" is Cree. It is
not French. In fact, it's been asked of me by a certain kind Moony-ass whom I love dearly, "What
on earth is a Dene?" even though they've lived for
years among and with them *and* among Cree of
northwestern Saskatchewan, where, as with northwestern Manitoba, the two languages meet. All
those years, they were under the impression that
these people were one and the very same, who
spoke the same language, which they are not and
which they don't. The two languages don't even
come from the same linguistic family and so are as
different from each other as chalk from cheese. For
instance, "come here" in Cree is "aastam"; in Dene
it is "goosi-gaal." "Lard" in Cree is "pimi"; in Dene,
it is "th'less," with a liberal amount of saliva sieved
through the tongue and teeth as they press against
each other at the apostrophe, which is tricky for
non-Dene speakers to pronounce. Ditto for a word

like "koo'lth-sli," which is Dene for "Oh, good grief" or "Oh, go on," while in Cree, it is the much more pronounceable "Neeeee."

BEFORE I SLIDE INTO THE WARP AND WEAVE of the trio of mythologies, I will have to give a crash course on Indigenous languages, though, thank God, only a brief one. That is, it will take nowhere near the eighteen years of pure toil and pleasure it took me to learn your beloved English. And French (c'est vrai), Italian (e vero), and music, that is to say, the language of Brahms and Chopin, one that I speak with complete fluency. And good portions of still others. Life father, like son, a fact of which I am extremely proud. Here goes...

Linguists inform us that there exist on this planet some seven thousand languages. The proliferation of dialects negates all hope of pinning down a number, but there you have it, a figure high enough to encourage those people who speak one language only, for now, to consider learning at least one other. Two of these umpteen languages, in any case, are spoken by more than one billion people each: Mandarin and English. Others are spoken by hundreds of millions: Spanish among them,

Arabic another. Or millions or thousands or hundreds or even just eight, like Busuu, a language in Cameroon on Central Africa's Atlantic coast, at least so linguists tell us.

Then there are the one hundred or so Indigenous languages that exist, or rather existed until recently, in Canada. And "existed" is the word, for more than two-thirds of the more than seventy Indigenous languages still living are in danger of dying, thanks to the internet and television. To give you an idea of their precarious status today, the Indigenous language most spoken, Cree, has but some ninety thousand speakers as of this writing. At the other end of the spectrum, one of Canada's seven Iroquoian languages, Tuscarora, recently lost its last fluent speaker when Helen Salter of the Six Nations First Nation outside Brantford, Ontario, died at ninety-three on December 2, 2020. So time is of the essence when it comes to preserving Cree, as is the case with other Indigenous languages. Who knows? God forbid, but this book may well be the last record of the world view and wisdom contained inside it.

If the twenty-four official European languages can be divided into three broad language families, with sub-groupings, then the one hundred

Indigenous languages that exist, or once existed, in North America can be divided into twelve language families. And of those twelve language families, I will single out only the main ones. The sheer number of Indigenous languages and dialects in British Columbia's challenging landscape, where mountain ranges have isolated communities one from the other for millennia, negates their inclusion. This leaves us with the four main families I wish to include here, if only for the context they give to my mother tongue of Cree. Those four linguistic families? Athapaskan, Iroquoian, Siouan, and Algonquian.

The people whose language belongs to the Athapaskan family of languages mostly inhabit the Yukon and the Northwest Territories. Dene is a member of this family. With Dene territory abutting and even straddling the northernmost tip of our three prairie provinces (and thus Cree territory), Dene is the most southerly of the Athapaskan languages, at least here in Canada (for there are some in the U.S.). The term "Dene," which means "people" in that language, can be confusing for some — it denotes both a language and the linguistic family it comes from. Slavey, whose land encircles the Northwest Territory's Great Bear Lake, is another Athapaskan language, as is Gwi'chin, through whose land passes that same territory's magnificent Mackenzie River at about its middle. This linguistic family also makes a quantum leap all the way to such southwestern American states as New Mexico, Arizona, and even California in the form of Navajo, Apache, and Comanche, thus hinting at some fascinating migration patterns of times long past.

The Iroquoian languages inhabit Southern Ontario and eastern Quebec, and then spill over into northern New York State to connect from there with other Iroquoian languages, such as Cherokee, which spread even farther southward into states such as North and South Carolina. The seven Iroquoian tongues spoken in Canada — for there are more in the U.S. — are Tuscarora, Mohawk, Cayuga, Oneida, Onondaga, Seneca, and what was once called Huron but, since 1999, has been called Wendat.

As for the Siouan linguistic family, member Nations include the Stoney, whose homeland lies in the foothills of southwestern Alberta just west of Calgary; the Assiniboine, whose territory straddles southern Saskatchewan and the American states of Idaho and Montana; the Lakota (of the Teton subgrouping); and the Dakota (of the Yankton and

Santee subgroupings), whose territory straddles the Saskatchewan-Manitoba border and the American states of North and South Dakota, Wisconsin, Nebraska, Minnesota, and even Montana.

The largest Indigenous language family, which also has the distinction of being the most alive, most spoken, among them all, is Algonquian. This family includes languages that are spoken in territory that covers most of the northern half of Canada's ten provinces, including Newfoundland when you factor in Labrador, which is Innu territory. There is a crucial distinction here: Algon*quian* is a linguistic family; Algon*quin* is a language within that family that is spoken mostly in southern and western Quebec along its border with Northeastern Ontario, as well as just north and just south of Ottawa.

As with the Iroquoian and Siouan language families, a goodly chunk of the Algonquian languages, too, spill over into the U.S. Ojibway territory, for instance, which in Canada hugs for the most part the northern extremity of the five Great Lakes, spills southward into Michigan, Wisconsin, Minnesota, and North Dakota, while sister language Abenaki, whose territory lies in southeastern Quebec near its border with New Hampshire, spills over into that state as well as its neighbour Vermont. Other Algonquian languages such as Maliseet (mostly New Brunswick) and Mi'kmaq (mostly Nova Scotia), too, bear kinships with Algonquian languages in New England states such as Maine, Massachusetts, and Rhode Island, connecting there with still other related Algonquian languages such as Wampanoag, Penobscot, Narragansett, and Pequot, right down to the state of Connecticut and its famous Pequot-owned Foxwoods Casino. As for Blackfoot, yet another Algonquian language, it straddles most vividly the Alberta–Montana border. So with Inuktitut spilling over into Alaska (the U.S.), Greenland (Denmark), and Siberia (Russia), and Athapaskan languages being spoken in Alaska, New Mexico, Arizona, and California, Cree and Algonquin end up holding pride of place as the only Indigenous languages that are uniquely and exclusively Canadian.

Also, and most explicitly, an Algonquian language, Cree lays claim to the lion's share of Canada. It is spoken in the northwestern tip of British Columbia and across almost all of Alberta, Saskatchewan, Manitoba, the northern half of Ontario, and the middle third of Quebec. And then there is dialect. As with languages the whole world over, Cree teems with dialects that are, in the end, uncountable. From the northwestern tip of British Columbia to the Atlantic coast of Quebec (and even Newfoundland, if you include Labrador), where Innu is an eastern extension of Cree — or Cree is a western extension of Innu, depending on your perspective — the dialects of the same basic language are spread so far out and are so numerous that they are mutually incomprehensible from one end of the country to the other. They might as well be two — or three or four or thirty — different languages. A Cree from Northern Alberta, for instance, doesn't understand a Cree from the James Bay coast of Quebec who doesn't understand an Innu of Labrador, just as an Argentinian doesn't understand a Cuban who doesn't understand a Peruvian who doesn't understand an Andalusian (just one dialect of many in Spain) when the four, in fact, are all speaking Spanish. Or an English Canadian doesn't understand a Texan who doesn't understand a Jamaican who doesn't understand a Northern Irishman when all four, in fact, are speaking English. Well, so it is with Cree. In northwestern Manitoba, for example, I can tell which village or First Nation a Cree-speaking person comes from just by the way they bend their vowels.

Cree is divided into four broad dialects: the Y dialect, the N dialect, the L dialect, and the TH dialect (with the hard "th" as in "though," as opposed to the soft as in "thought"). And that's my dialect, the dialect spoken in the land I come from: Northern Manitoba where it meets Northern Saskatchewan. And this is the dialect of Cree I will use as my foundation in this book.

AT SEVENTY, I STILL SPEAK CREE, as I will to the end of my days. If anything, I speak it with a fluency and rapidity that make some people marvel at the syllables' rhythm, which is musical, but even more at its speed, which is blinding. Cree is the fastest language in the world to begin with, but so fast do I speak it that lip-readers from far maameek have been known to go cross-eyed for entire days at a stretch just from trying to read my lips. There are two words for "south" in Cree. The first, "sawanook," means the cardinal direction. The second, "maameek," also means the cardinal direction but, moreover, connotes, in a very subtle way, social standing just one step down from us Cree, as in "the south where live those Moony-ass." I think in Cree, dream in it, write books and plays and music in it (that is, as lyrics to songs I write for my Kurt Weill–inspired cabaret shows that tell Cree stories). I speak, what's more, the dialect of the language that is spoken in the most remote corner of northwestern Manitoba. My people, thus, are a subarctic people — not quite Arctic, for that great honour goes to the laughter-loving Inuit. Still, we are close enough to them in terms geographic to be their kin, for our peoples intermarried at various points in our histories. By the grace of such unions, in spite of their rarity, I have relatives who are part Inuit; that's how northern a people we are.

Regardless, Cree was the lingua franca in the Highway household when I was growing up. It was only with later generations that it started fading. The cause? Electricity and its most subversive offspring, television — and later, the internet. The very first victim of this "offspring" was our language and, in fact, all Native languages across this country. Television ushered in the era of their gradual erasure. The first casualty of this linguistic loss? Laughter. For if Cree is the world's fastest language, it is also its funniest. The reason? A clown god motors our Native languages, making them doubly spectacular, doubly joyful. It certainly does with Cree. A laughing deity virtually governs the

way our tongues move, the way our blood flows,
the way our lungs pump, the way our brains pop,
dance, and sizzle. Called Weesaa-geechaak in
Cree, Nanabush in Ojibway, Glooscap in Mi'kmaq,
Coyote in British Columbia's southern interior,
Raven on its coast, Iktomi — a being half-human
and half-spider — among the Lakota and the Dakota
of Southern Manitoba, Southern Saskatchewan,
and the Dakotas of the northern U.S., that being
is known in English as the Trickster. So when the
generation that followed mine stopped speaking
Cree, half their sense of humour disappeared. It got
watered down by the English language. Fortunately
for me, electricity didn't arrive in my hometown
of old Brochet until the summer of 1973, when
I was twenty-one, too late for me to lose my language, which is how and why my Cree survived
unscathed. Ooski-p'mat-sak (the new livers, i.e.,
the next generation) were not so lucky. So they
laughed with half our usual gusto. They chuck-
led, yes, once every Tuesday when the priest wasn't
looking. They chortled, they giggled, they snick-
ered, they snorted, they squeaked, they squawked,
keegi-thagi-pathi-wak, keewee-cheegi-pathi-wak,
but guffaw robustly until they farted they did not.
Suddenly, farting was criminal, a capital offence for

which one could spend a year in prison. The nerve! "Without that language," the Trickster might very well say, "laughter dies."

As for all the languages the whole world over, they are so different one from the other that the result, if they were all spoken at once, would be a cacophony, a dreadful clattering of wayward consonants. Still, all are here for a reason. Each has its genius, its strength, its applicability. Most pointedly, if botanists tell us that the Amazon jungle has plants and herbs that number in the millions, each of which holds the key to a possible cure for physical ailments, illness, and disease, then languages function likewise. The difference is that the ailments they address are not so much physical as emotional, psychological, and spiritual, ailments that can be just as debilitating, just as lethal. Without languages we would be lost, directionless, even suicidal. Life on Earth would be static; it would have no meaning. Like birdsong, languages make our planet a beautiful place, a fascinating place — indeed, a miraculous place — to live on.

TWO

ON CREATION

ONE WINTER NIGHT SOME FORTY YEARS AGO, a most unruly and spectacular celebration was transpiring in a room at a hotel in downtown Toronto. Unfortunately, at the time, I was ignorant of this signal event and so missed its madness, one that mounted as the evening progressed, or so they say. Then again, isn't this the case with all celebrations? The madness mounts as the libations amass? It certainly is in the Native community. What makes our parties doubly unruly, however, and therefore doubly spectacular, is the fact that a clown god lives inside us. A spirit half-human and half-god, as is the case with all superheroes in all world mythologies. The difference is that our Trickster has a sense of humour and a concupiscence that know no limit.

So wild and unruly was the party I speak of that unexpected visitors arrived at the door in a manner...well...unexpected.

The thing was that my dear friend and colleague — Billy Boy Cut Throat, we shall call him, for the purpose of concealing his true identity — had been fuelling the event with a liberal supply of some magical tobacco he always seemed to have on his person throughout those years, a substance that, by the way, is much more conducive to the health of Indigenous communities across this country than alcohol has ever been. But back to this mystical t'steemow (tobacco) — true to the nature of this trance-inducing substance, the party was rocking and rolling and raging and reeling when a rap on the door made talk stop and tension strike.

"Police!" shouted a reveller.

At the point in Canada's history that I describe here, while people were still allowed to smoke cigarettes — that is, cigarettes made of regular tobacco — inside hotel rooms in the 1970s, possession of the "drug" then known as "marijuana" or "weed" or "grass" was a criminal offence. You could be thrown in prison to languish therein for years, just for having one joint in your pocket. Fortunately for us all today, we can enjoy it openly and legally (though not in interior spaces such as hotel rooms). Unfortunately for my dear friend and colleague Billy Boy Cut Throat, he was forced by circumstance to engage in an act that transformed him into a myth — if not instantly, then over the course of the next three years. What did he do? The "drug" was so incendiary, so unsafe to have on one's person, that he rushed to the window, pried it open with his usual panache, and jumped to his death. At least, that is what most eyewitnesses were under the impression he had just done — killed himself — for he was never seen again, or so went the gossip from one end of the land to the other. (It didn't help that a good half of the guests in that room were stoned out of their minds.) To add fuel to the fire (as is the way in our culture), the story was embellished to include the fact that our hero had jumped from a floor unheard of in the annals of history Indigenous — it was the thirtieth, so of course he died.

In Cree, there are three words for the idea of narrative. The first, "aachi-moowin," means "to tell a story," that is, "to tell the truth." The second, "kithaas-kiwin," means "to tell a lie," that is, "to weave a web of fiction." And at a point exactly halfway between these two polar opposites stands "achi-thoogee-win," which means "to mythologize," that is, "to weave a web of magic."

As I wandered across Ontario over the next three years (the job I had then entailed such activity), I traced this story from city to reserve to town and back to city, believing all along that Billy Boy Cut Throat had plunged to his death, that Billy Boy Cut Throat's "spirit," one known for its strength, its lust, its indomitability, clung to a window ledge outside that window "for hours," while the law enforcers turned the room inside out looking for evidence of criminal activity of the sort for which Billy Boy Cut Throat had gained, through the years, such glamorous notoriety. Over time, the thirtieth floor in that hotel room became the twenty-fifth, then the twentieth, then the fifteenth, then the tenth, and so on, until, some three years later, I finally ran into Mr. Cut Throat himself, live and in the flesh and in full control of his faculties, in his home community in Northwestern Ontario some six hundred kilometres north of the fabled city of Thunder Bay on Great Lake Superior's tempestuous shores. By the time I got to the source of the myth that electrified my imagination every time I thought of it, as it did for so many others, it turned out that the downtown Toronto hotel room had not been on the thirtieth nor the twentieth nor the tenth nor the seventh nor even the third. It had been on the second! And Billy Boy Cut Throat hadn't hung on to that window ledge "for hours"; he had merely dropped to the ground, suffered a few minor scrapes and one sore ankle, then hobbled off down the alleyway, around the corner, and down the street to the nearest bar. That was the truth. That was the non-fiction. That was aachi-moowin.

That the floor was the thirtieth was the lie. That was the fiction. That was outright kithaas-kiwin.

At a point exactly halfway between these two conflicting narratives, or the two versions of the same story — that is, a point exactly halfway between the truth and the lie — sits the narrative I heard from perhaps the tenth teller of the tale, a good three years before I caught up with my friend up north. By this tenth telling of the story, I had it firmly planted inside my mind — in my subconscious, in my dream world: plain, old, ordinary human being Billy Boy Cut Throat had not only sprung the fingernails of Superman himself, but he had also sprouted the wings of an angel, which was how he had managed to hover Holy Spirit–like high up in the air outside that window on what in my wildest imaginings was the ninetieth floor of some miraculous hotel room in downtown Toronto. If an angel is a kind of divinity, a kind of half-man/half-god, then so was my friend Billy Boy Cut Throat that night. That was the myth. That was achi-thoogee-win. That was the magic.

And that is precisely the region of our collective dream world, our collective subconscious, where men sprout wings, horses sprout wings, creatures half-man and half-horse walk this Earth; that is the region of our lives where exist beings who are half-man and half-goat, half-woman and half-fish, half-man and half-coyote, half-woman and half-spider, where snakes talk to women (but not to men), women give birth without having had sex, dead men rise from the grave, where men — and women, too — are half-human and half-divine. And an old man in the sky with a fearsome scowl and a long white beard can part Lake Ontario right down the middle with a wave of his golden thunderbolt so that Ontarians can go shopping in Rochester, New York, without first having to pass through Buffalo, New York, or Gananoque, Ontario, or even Toronto's Pearson Airport, and anyone who dares to pursue them drowns in the waters of a heartless lake. And that's how my dear weechee-waagan (friend) Billy Boy Cut Throat, from the wilds of

Northwestern Ontario, got transformed from a man (the truth) to a god (the lie) but, in the end, was — and still is — both (the myth). Thus does he hover in the place where live such beings, that is, in the world of magic, in mythology.

All this leads us to the question: How did the place we know as the universe come into being? How did the planet known as Earth emerge from aachi-moowin, pass through kithaas-kiwin, and end up as achi-thoogee-win, thus becoming the miraculous environment that it is today? What kind of god or angel or combination thereof was responsible for its creation?

THE YOUNGEST OF THE THREE MYTHOLOGIES I discuss in this book is Christianity, the youngest in the sense that it came into its own only after its predecessors, the Greek and Roman systems, which we will call, for the sake of simplicity, classical mythology, had seen their glory. Certainly, the Christian way of thinking is the most familiar to the modern reader. Although the first parts of its great book of wisdom, namely the Old Testament, may have been written as early as the years between 1200 and 165 BCE, the New Testament didn't see the light of day until the first century CE, around the time when the Roman system, successor to that of ancient Greece, started fading into obsolescence. And those first five centuries of the new millennium marked the period when Christian mythology started taking ascendance in what would be a new world order, the one we know today.

The first point to note about this particular mythology is that the dream world it defines is monotheistic in structure, meaning it defines a monotheistic collective subconscious, a monotheistic universe. Again, the word comes to us from ancient Greek — "mono" meaning "one" and "theos" meaning "god" — to define a system of thought where exists but one god only. The god who arrived in the "New World" in 1492 came alone; he showed no sign of having a wife, a girlfriend, or even a mistress, meaning he never had sex. The second point is that this one god is male, and male exclusively. And heterosexual male, with not one speck of feminine attribute, physical, emotional, biological, or otherwise. The idea of divinity in female form is absent entirely from this system. The third point is that he is perfect, flawless; there is not one thing wrong with him. Omniscient, he has been called, and omnipotent, omnipresent, omni-this, omni-that, omni-everything—like Santa Claus, "he knows when you're awake; he knows if you've been bad or good." He knows everything, feels everything, can do everything, including putting an end to war, one would think. The fourth point is that he has been anthropomorphized by artists in paintings and sculptures, as well as by writers. Which is why we know this god as a scowling old man with an absorbent cotton beard, rearing from a swirl of angry clouds draped in what looks like a bedsheet and menacing us with a golden thunderbolt. The fifth point to note is that in this mythology, time is of the essence. Space, meaning the planet, the universe, our environment, meaning air, water, soil, vegetation, and all that sustains us, is of little to no consequence.

The sixth point is that Christian mythology defines a collective subconscious in which time is structured on, is governed and guided by, the principles of one straight line that travels from point A to point B to point C. In the beginning was this void, this endless soupy mass of matter that, according to respected American physicist Heinz Pagels in his landmark book *The Cosmic Code*, pulsated and danced and swirled through the great dome of space. From this great swirl of nothingness emerged a god, a kind of super-angel — a kind of super–Billy Boy Cut Throat — who, first of all, was male, and male exclusively, and second, who gave birth, by himself, seemingly with no need of partnership from or collaboration with a female, to the universe, with its planets and its stars and its moons, and the earth, with its soil and its rock and its water and its untold quadrillions of molecules. In the act of creating this universe, there was no sexual act between two partners, no physical pleasure, no extended period of pregnancy, no biological process remotely conceivable. *Poof*, the world just happened in six short days. That was the beginning of time, the beginning of that straight line, on the first day of which this male god gave birth(!) to light, on the second day to the atmosphere, and so on, until, on the sixth day, he created man from a little ball of mud and woman from his rib bone. Apparently unnecessary to the act of creation, woman came as an afterthought.

And the narrative goes on from there, the most salient feature being that this male "angel" — for his counterpart in hell, too, was once an angel — this male god gave man the power to rule over nature, to exploit it, and to do with it as he pleased. The midpoint of that straight line is when this god's only son, a being half-divine and half-human (and also male), like Billy Boy Cut Throat, appears on the earth, and on a very specific part of the earth, one might add, with the purpose in mind of teaching human beings truth, love, and humble forgiveness, a project not entirely successful, it would seem, if one is to judge by events today in that part of the world. And at the end of that straight line comes Armageddon, the destruction of the universe, by this same angel, this same god: the end of the earth, the end of time. Inspired by South Dakota—born Oglala Lakota writer Vine Deloria Jr. in his landmark book *God Is Red*, I like to refer to that mythology's great book of wisdom, its great book of magic, by calling this cryptic conceit the Book-of-Genesis-to-the-Book-of-Revelation straight line.

And, last, this male god gave us this earth as a gift. And then snatched it away. The narrative of eviction from a garden because of a woman's engagement in an act of pleasure—the eating of an apple—is one that, so far as I know, exists in three mythologies and three only—Christian, Judaic, and Islamic—not coincidentally, the world's three largest monotheistic mythologies. Space, in other words—the garden of Eden, the planet called

Earth — was given to us and then taken away. Put another way, the umbilical cord that connected us to our mother, the Earth, was cut. And time is our curse. In that system, we don't live in the here and now; we don't belong here; rather, we float about somewhere in a state of pure theory called "chronology," an arrow of time that hurtles ever forward, day by day by day, straight to an ending called Armageddon.

When I went for a recent walk with my daughter and her two children to the south bank of the Ottawa River, where it widens out to a full-sized lake, a five-minute stroll from where I live with my lifelong partner, her biological father, we stood on the shoreline to gaze at the sunset. There before us, my two grandchildren, aged eight and ten, were splashing about on the melting spring ice in their little rubber boots, silhouetted against the pink and purple of the last rays of daylight. My daughter said to me in total earnest, "I don't think that Marek and Milena will ever have children." What she was really saying was: "I think we've arrived at the end." And it's true: beautiful as it is, the Ottawa River is already dying. Because of industries such as pulp and paper upstream, it is radioactive.

· · ·

THE SECOND MYTHOLOGY UNDER discussion here differs dramatically on all these points. Greek mythology, though born more or less during the same period as Christianity, bloomed much faster and died much sooner. Around the seventh century BCE is the period generally given by archaeologists for its birth, though one can surmise that its gestation period would have started some centuries prior. Greek mythology, first of all, defines a collective subconscious that is polytheistic in structure. Humanity and the universe were created by many ("poly") gods ("theos"). In this universe, that is to say, there exists not just one but many gods. And many, many goddesses. In other words, this system has room, and plenty of it, for the idea of divinity in female form. An epidemic of divine fecundity far too active, and far too exciting, to give fair treatment in a chapter as brief as this; suffice to say that, in this dream world, there was a god of the sky, a goddess of the Earth, a god of this, a goddess of that, a goddess of wisdom, a goddess of love, a god of death. In fact, there seems to be not a single twitch of the human organism and of nature for which the Greeks didn't have a god or a goddess. Trees were divinities named Dryads, rivers were goddesses known as Naiads, reeds by the river were gods, sound was a cute little nymph called, in Greek as in English, Echo, one not seen but heard. There were the Muses, there were the Fates, the Graces, the Pleiades...

The creation of the Earth, and of the universe, moreover, was the result of a patently physical, biological act by an ancient male god whom few have ever heard of, but who some accounts say was a wind called Ophion, a wind who wound his immense physicality around a female force of energy called Eurynome, which copulative connection gave birth to the universe, with its stars and its moons and its planets, including one that eventually came to be known as Earth. The goddess Eurynome was a female entity who eventually came to be known by the Greeks as Gaia, precursor to other Mother Earth goddess figures through the centuries and eventually to the Mother Earth goddess known as Hera. And Mother Earth Hera mated with Father Sky Zeus. The universe and its contents, in other words, were born out of an act of sex, an act of patent biological and pleasurable reality. The king of all these deities, god of the sky Zeus, like the Christian god, brandishes a golden thunderbolt, *but* he has a wife, Hera. And they enjoy sex with vim and with vigour, and so have children, two being Hephaestus, the god of black-smiths and artisans (Vulcan in Roman mythology), and Ares, the god of war (Mars). Which doesn't nullify the fact that they still fight and quarrel. The reason? Here's one example — to Hera's great ire, Zeus was notorious for having sex, with too much vim and too much vigour. Outside his marriage *and* with genders other than women. Hera, for example, traumatized the Earth with her great fits of jealousy when she got wind of the fact that her husband, Zeus-in-the-guise-of-swan, had "ravished" (read: raped) a princess of Sparta named Leda, to name but one of Zeus's innumerable "ravishments." From this union, the human princess subsequently gave birth to a half-goddess/half-woman whom we all know as Helen of Troy.

And in their "horrible numerosity" (to quote Henry James), the lives of the gods and goddesses in this dream world were overseen by an original pantheon of twelve who lived in an ancient Greek version of heaven. This was Mount Olympus, an actual mountain, still there today, in the north of the country toward the modern-day Greek city of Thessaloniki. Still, these deities have one thing in common with the Christian god: they, too, were anthropomorphized through years of development by painters, sculptors, and poets. Hermes, the messenger/Trickster god, for example, is an athletic young man who flies by means of wings on his sandals and wears a helmet that holds magic powers. Dionysus is a celebratory god who drinks wine at liberty and with great gusto. Artemis, the huntress; Athena, goddess of war and of wisdom; Aphrodite, goddess of love; Poseidon, god of the sea; Hades, god of the afterlife — all have their physical appearances, an item of clothing, or a weapon that defines them. Poseidon, in his best-known portrayal, for example, rears out of the sea in a chariot dragged by a winged horse named Pegasus, his son by Medusa, the snake-haired Gorgon. Brandishing a trident, just like a certain evil "king" who reigns over the afterlife in Christian mythology, he rides the foam as though on a surfboard. And Aphrodite wears a magic golden girdle that inspires passion in both immortals and mortals.

Magnificent as they are, however, none of the gods or goddesses this dream world teems with is perfect; they all have real emotions; they all have genuine physical sensations, desires, frailties, and flaws, just like real-life, four-dimensional, flesh-and-blood human beings. These were gods of pleasure; they got angry, yes, and they fought here, there, and everywhere, just like humans, but what they were here for was a good time, a grand celebration of the fact of nature, of biology, and its wondrous inner workings.

Depending on the history of any given state — invasion, war, extended periods of peace, alliances, epidemics, pandemics — some mythologies have swallowed others to become a sort of super-mythology. As Greek political, economic, and military power waned over the course of the third millennium BCE to give way to Roman ascendance, so did its mythology. Thus it was that Father Sky Zeus was subsumed by his Roman successor, Jupiter, Mother Earth Hera by Rome's Juno, and all the other deities were likewise transformed, if in name only: Hermes to Mercury, Artemis to Diana, Dionysus to Bacchus, and so on. Then, as the Roman Empire started crumbling through the first and second centuries CE, Christian mythology rose in influence to replace Jupiter with the biblical Jehovah, who gradually became Yahweh, who became the male god being addressed today when a member of the faithful says, "Our Father, Who art in heaven…"

By the dawn of the first millennium CE, then, the idea of the goddess had started fading to the point where only faint echoes of ancient Greece's and ancient Rome's polytheistic systems remain in Christian mythology. Drastically demoted, the Greek and Roman gods and goddesses, pleasure principles every one of them, linger in the only too human and only too tortured forms of Catholic saints. Saint Sebastian, with his arrow-pierced, bleeding body; Saint Lawrence, who was roasted naked and alive on a fiery grill, thus earning his title as patron saint of cooks and chefs; kind Saint Cecilia, who, in a sense, is the "muse" of music; and compassionate Saint Veronica — all have their penitents, their faithful, but at least, feminists would say, a good half of them were female. Still, none is a god. And none is a goddess. Even the Virgin Mary, frequently invoked like a goddess in the most fervent of Catholic cultures, is not — she is a woman; she is human. In the Christian system, only one god remains; all the others were wiped off the map — by human politics. And that is the god who arrived on the shores of what is now the Bahamas in October 1492.

Brandishing a thunderbolt he had stolen from the Roman King of the Gods, Jupiter, who, in turn, had lifted it from ancient Greece's King of the Gods, Zeus, he stepped off Christopher Columbus's

Santa Maria, and, angry as hell, thundered, "I am the only god!" Why was he so angry? Well, wouldn't you be angry if you hadn't had sex in a thousand years? The thunderbolt flashed, its thunder cracked, and the newly crowned King of the Gods continued, "Anyone who dares worship another god will be destroyed." No wonder Mom, a diehard Catholic from age one day, was terrified of lightning. To appease its wrath, she would run out in the deluge to hang her rosary from the highest tree she could find in the immediate vicinity of our summer residence, a canvas tent. Except that in subarctic climes the trees are not very tall, because in that area we are getting close to the treeline. The treeline? That region of the world where trees stop growing, to be taken over by the tundra, treeless land — what we call "the barrens" — that sweeps clean across the length of Nunavut right to the North Pole and even through Siberia on the earth's other side, a breathtaking vista no matter how many times you see it.

My father, Joe Highway, was tall and stately — he looked like a king — but my mother, Balazee Highway, was short and elfin. And very funny. Though much prettier, she looked like Granny from the television series *The Beverly Hillbillies.* Thankfully, the trees we had were short as well, which meant one thing — drenched to the bone by driving rain, Mom didn't have to reach very high to hang her rosary from the apex of the tree, generally a spruce. And her Catholic faith stood her in good stead, for she lived to the ripe old age of eighty-eight and never once got struck by God's bolt of lightning. Taap'wee. Maw weegaach neetha nigi-thaaskin. (It's true. I never lie.)

In Greek mythology, or in its story of creation, there was no sense of time — or at least no all-pervasive, obsessive sense of it. Nature came to fruition — as propelled by these divinities, forces of nature every one of them — in no particular order; it just flourished, over an unspecified period of time, as one great act of pleasure, one great act of spectacular beauty. Space was much more important than time. And by space, I mean the land, the air, the water. Therefore, Greek mythology doesn't function according to the rigours of one straight line, with a beginning of time, time in the middle, and the end of time, nor does it function like a complete circle, but rather more like a circle interrupted and, thus, a curve, a sort of grand semicircle. And the reason for this interruption is because of what happened — politically, historically, militarily — in that part of the world around the time of the birth of Christ, that point in time when Roman civilization — and thus Roman mythology — had taken over from the Greeks, and Christian mythology, in its turn, came to supplant Roman mythology. For mythologies, it would seem — as with the gods and goddesses that live therein — have limited lifespans, limited periods of relevance; they are born, they flourish, they fade, they die. Which is where new gods — and/or goddesses — spring from a battlefield covered, all too often, in blood, ashes, and empty hulks of temples, of churches.

I travel the world. I am now of an age where I can say that I have visited sixty-three countries. Born a nomad — into a caribou-hunting culture — always a nomad. I've lived in Europe for twenty-one years: one in England, fourteen in France (winters only), and six in Italy (ditto). I've criss-crossed France, Spain, Germany, Finland, Demark, and several countries in Eastern Europe and loved every second of the experience. But I have always been struck by this stark reality: all these countries have all these churches. Truly spectacular cathedrals, each holding untold riches, some of them so ornate in their construction that it took hundreds of years to build them. And they're cavernous. St. Peter's Basilica in Rome alone has room for sixty thousand standing worshippers. When these Roman Catholic cathedrals were built, anytime between the tenth and seventeenth centuries, Christianity was at its height, its most fervent. When you stand inside these buildings today, the faith that existed back then is palpable. This sense of awe fills your spirit.

But now they're empty. A very lonely-looking and very old priest will be holding a Mass at, say, the Basilica di Maria della Salute on the Grand Canal in Venice. The space has room for more than two thousand people. The Sunday morning I was there, twelve creaky old nuns were kneeling at the pews at the front, their quavering, feeble, ancient voices wafting like thistles to the sky-high ceiling. At the Vatican, St. Peter's Basilica is overrun not with sincere worshippers but with tourists taking selfies beside statues of saints or tombs of popes. The French will tell you that God died in France in the seventeenth century — that is, the Age of Enlightenment. In Eastern Europe, these spectacular churches are now upscale restaurants and giant discos, while the smaller chapels are hair salons or shops selling luxury goods.

In northern Canada today, few Catholic priests are under the age of eighty. And the seminaries are empty. When I was a boy, reserves used to have a priest and a brother. Now five reserves share one priest, and a very old priest at that, and no brother. Exhausted from flying forbiddingly long distances by bush plane from one northern reserve to another, a priest is lucky if he gets to say five Masses on five different, widely spaced reserves on five different Sundays. So who says the Masses when the priest is absent? The women. Untrained, unlicensed, even illiterate, and they are forbidden to touch the Eucharist — the body of Christ in the form of a host, a coin-sized wafer of unleavened bread — *because* they are women. Yet they say the Masses, hear confessions, serve communion, and officiate at weddings, baptisms, and funerals.

When I was a boy, the feast called Christmas was all about Jesus. On ordinary Sundays, we altar boys at the Guy Hill Indian Residential School in northern Manitoba would be four in number, wearing black cassocks and white surplices, rather pedestrian when it came to a Catholic church service. But at special services such as Christmas midnight Mass, we would be a dozen, from the youngest at six to the oldest at fifteen, floating about like angels in our scarlet cassocks, florid white surplices embroidered with silk thread, with kite-sized scarlet satin bows bursting from our necks, assisting

Father Remy, the school principal, aglow in his white satin chasuble and damask embroidery. The altar, with its umpteen tall white candles, stood on a raised dais covered with a white taffeta ceremonial cloth bordered in lace, graced by the golden chalice that held Christ's blood (the wine), the golden ciborium that held his body (the hosts for communicants), the golden thurible that bore incense from which smoke billowed its intoxicating fragrance, the golden this, the golden that, all while a two-hundred-voice choir — one hundred girls, one hundred boys — sang in four-part harmony of angels, of shepherds, of cows, of donkeys, of a manger with its infant, a boy named Jesus. He and he alone was the focus of all this attention.

Today, the sacred holiday is about an old white man with a big white beard and a belly the size of a stove, flying around the world on a sled pulled by nine flying reindeer. Christmas trees, dancing snowmen, presents, candy canes — candy, candy, and yet more candy — you name it, but there is not a single sign in all that circus of the Son of God. Or his birth.

Same with Easter. At the Guy Hill Indian Residential School, the celebration of Holy Week, the week leading up to Easter, started with Palm

Sunday, when Jesus enters Jerusalem surrounded by people waving branches from palm trees, and we were all given palms to hold through the service; Good Friday, when Jesus in the guise of Father Remy washed the feet of one of his apostles, in this case, the school janitor, say, or a teacher or a brother; the Stations of the Cross, when we altar boys would follow our Lord on High around the entire circumference of the school's church, bewailing the weight of his cross, wanting to help him, and weeping — yes, literally weeping — suffering with him at every stop he made on his way up the hill to his death. All this was topped by a midnight Mass even more spectacular than the one at Christmas, as it led up to the morning of the miracle, the one that underpins the entire superstructure that is Christian monotheism: the Lord's resurrection. We were in awe.

Today, Easter is about a rabbit who lays eggs made of chocolate and hides them from children in lawns and gardens. What does that say about the status of the central hero figure in a certain dream world, in a certain collective subconscious? When he is upstaged by a rabbit? Who lays eggs?

Whatever the fate, recent or soon to be recent, of Christian mythology, the fate of Greek mythology

is better known, if only because it faded into obsolescence over the course of a half millennium some
1,500 years ago, thus putting it in a place where we
can examine it with the objectivity provided by
distance. As for paradise or the Garden of Eden,
the closest thing the Greeks had was a place called
Arcadia. Still extant and a province in the country
that we know in modern times as Greece, it is situated in the Peloponnese peninsula south of Athens,
a mountainous region with extensive grassland.
And it is beautiful. *And* it has rabbits, though ones
incapable of laying eggs, so far as is known.

The day I was there one mid-October was sun-
kissed, balmy, and breezy, conducive to napping,
which is what I was doing when I was woken by
bells clanging from the necks of sheep being herded
homeward and onward by a very attractive god
called Pan, or so I was dreaming. And so he was.
That shepherd, for shepherd my "god" turned out
to be, was aged not one day past twenty, was built
like a gymnast, and had lips like wine. That's what
happens when dream merges into reality: the magic
called myth transpires.

The ancient Greeks were not here to suffer;
humankind was not kicked out of the garden of
joy, that great space of pleasure, the garden of

fleshly desires, by an angry male god. Rather, that space was a gift from a benevolent — well, mostly benevolent — female god known as Mother Earth, a garden so very beautiful that one god from among the great pantheon of twelve forsook his residence on the airy heights of Mount Olympus to come and live, instead, a life of pleasure — including gallons of sex — right there in the garden called Arcadia: half-goat, half-man — and therefore with hooves that were cloven like those of a certain evil angel from Christian mythology — an exciting, excitable, perpetually sexually aroused deity named Pan, from which comes the English word for "panic," only in this context, the kind of "panic of pleasure" one feels when sex is in sight and the liquids of love begin their dance...right there, smack in the middle of the garden.

The Greeks weren't here to apologize for meriting eviction from a garden "because of an act of pleasure indulged in by a woman," which I would learn in catechism class at the Guy Hill Indian Residential School was the definition of the idea of "original sin." Our teacher, a skeletal young priest with orange hair that looked like shredded wheat, would tap his long wooden pointer here and there on the blackboard behind him, showing us the apple, showing us the snake, showing us the woman — the idea of "original sin" appeared to excite him, for he licked his lips — and making us sing, "In the great hereafter, oh Lord of lords, we'll see you there." Only years later would I learn that the "great hereafter" the pink-skinned priest spoke of was, in fact, a time of pure and utter theory — it did not exist. The ancient Greeks, I would learn even more years later, lived not in the then but in the now. And here in Canada, and only after years of plumbing the depths of Indigenous spirituality, I add my own words: "This space, our Earth, is *now*. It is heaven; it is hell. It's what you make it *while* you're here."

AND THAT BRINGS US TO THE THIRD, and oldest, mythology under discussion, which is North American Indigenous mythology. In Indigenous mythology, there exists not one God, as in Christian mythology; not many gods, as in Greek mythology; but, rather, the concept of "God in all" or "God in everything." Not monotheistic, not polytheistic, North American Indigenous mythology is, by contrast, pantheistic in structure. A pantheistic divinity created the universe: "pan" meaning "all" in ancient Greek, and "theos," of course, meaning "god." This system comes to us from a time before humankind began conceiving of divinity as having human form. Divine energy, in this system, has not been anthropomorphized. Not having left nature, it still lives inside and with it. All of nature — from leaves to soil to water to the dog lolling lazily about on your living room carpet to the heart inside your body to the beloved inside your life — virtually pulsates with divinity. A leaf on a tree, a blade of grass, a fish in the river, that ray of sunlight that filters in through your kitchen window and falls on your arm, the wind that moves through your lungs, thus giving movement to your heart and veins and brain — all are divine energies, divine beings with a living, breathing soul. In Cree and other Algonquian languages, the world is Mantoo, meaning Spirit, not a ghost but an energy. Or K'si-mantoo (Great Spirit). Moony-ass speakers, god bless them, have come to pronounce and spell the latter as "Gitche Manitou." Divinity in a pantheistic system is conceived of not as a man or a woman, as in the monotheistic and polytheistic systems, but rather as an electric bolt of energy — a premonition of Zeus and God the Father's golden thunderbolt perhaps? — that shoots through the universe, animating all that it passes through. If mythologists, theologists, and cosmologists call this principle pantheism, or "god in all," then cellular biologists call it animism, or "soul in all," from the Latin word "animus," which means "soul." Pantheism, that is to say, has its roots planted firmly in biological reality: according to its structure, or its system, a bird has a soul, a rock has a soul, a woman has a soul. Which is not the case in monotheism. In monotheism, a tree is an "it," a rock is an "it," and, for all the dignity bestowed on her, a woman might as well be an "it." To push that question just one step further, a woman giving birth without having had sex? A male god giving birth to a planet by himself — that is, without collaboration from a feminine force? That is truth biological? That is biology? I don't think so.

Indigenous accounts of creation vary widely across the continent, as they did in ancient Greece, as they did in the ancient Middle East, but the general consensus, at least in Cree stories, is that the universe and its contents came into being as the result of the efforts of a female force of energy known as Omaa-maa. The Cree word for mother is "maamaa"; nimaamaa, kimaamaa, oomaa-maawa-wa: my mother, your mother, his/her mother.

Interestingly enough, moreover, in this particular account there appears to be no overwhelming evidence of masculine involvement in the process of procreation. This girl was endlessly sexual, endlessly sensual, endlessly fertile, a creature of pleasure, a creature of the flesh who gave birth, in no particular order, with no great fixation on the concept of time, to many, many most wondrous and most, most beautiful things...including, at the start of her narrative, this laughing, hysterically funny, totally outrageous, totally concupiscent clown called, in English, the Trickster — who is half-human and half-god, like all superheroes in all mythologies the whole world over, and like Billy Boy Cut Throat in our little tale of the madcap party in downtown Toronto.

Mother Earth also gave birth to women. And then men, as an afterthought, as they weren't necessary to the act of creation. And mosquitoes, by the way. And blackflies. And blood cells that don't quite always work out in the human bloodstream, causing fatal illnesses. She is far from perfect. Yes, she is beautiful; yes, she is grand. And she is generous, she is bountiful, she is kind and everloving and supportive and affectionate. But like the mother goddess Hera in Greek mythology, when tried to the limit by the masculine side of her that is not quite in working order, she can be one jealous, furiously angry force from hell. She destroys with earthquakes, she destroys with hurricanes, she destroys with famine and starvation and drought and war and with all kinds of ailments, physical, emotional, mental, and spiritual. But then she gives us trees, she gives us flowers, she gives us lakes, loons, red-winged blackbirds; she gives us sunsets and she gives us wind. In the end, Mother Earth is beautiful and terrible, kind and gentle, and so she is to be respected, revered, thanked.

On Reindeer Lake in Northern Manitoba, where my home village of Brochet sits like a cherry at its top, the first two weeks of August are a dream from heaven. When the summer is at its height, its waters are as kind as Jesus, its five thousand islands glimmer with a beauty so intense that its hurts the eyes to look upon them. Big Sandy Island, for instance — just inside the Manitoba border with Saskatchewan — is a two-kilometre-long crescent, shaped like a boomerang, little more than a sandbar, with powder-fine gold sand beaches on both its north and south sides. Flanked by small forests at both ends, it looks like a barbell. The summer I was five and the summer I was ten, we lived there.

Imagine camping with your parents for two months every summer in the most stunning place on Earth. Two months! As a nomadic people, we lived on different islands on Reindeer Lake, or on different lakes between that lake and the Nunavut border, a distance of some 250 kilometres with ten thousand lakes between them. And this being August, there are no bugs. And no people, just you and your family. That was Mother Earth at her most generous, her most loving. That's when you would hear her breathe, hear her hum.

But one kilometre to the west floated a much larger island, this one called Boundary Island because it straddled the Manitoba–Saskatchewan border. And beyond it stretched a huge expanse of open water with no islands, the only respite from which was Porcupine Point, jutting out from the mainland on the Saskatchewan side some ten kilometres away. We'd stand on this rock the size of a house at the far western tip of Boundary Island, my younger brother and I, and look with a mixture of longing and fear, because it was always a gamble to cross that span in our little ten-horsepower outboard motor before a wind swooped in from nowhere and, within seconds, with the might of a tornado, whipped the glass-smooth water into waves high as houses to drown us. Every summer there were drownings on that lake. My school friend Raphael Halkett, eighteen at the time, and his sixteen-year-old wife, Mary Rose, six months pregnant with their first child, were devoured by the might of stunning, omnivorous Reindeer Lake mere metres before they reached Brochet this one September. There on that shore, the two sets of parents wept in silence, for months. That was Mother Nature at her most cruel.

In another story, two young men of some thirty summers were crossing Reindeer Lake in October — *never* cross Reindeer Lake in October; that's when the wind is at its most powerful, the waves at their most treacherous — from island to mainland on another part of the lake, their canoe weighted down with their fishing nets, their intention to put them away for the season. With one hundred lead sinkers per net, small as adult human fingers but nonetheless each as heavy as a hammer, and at least fifty nets on board, the canoe was already near sinking when they started out. A wind came along, the waves got higher, the boat sank. The next morning, or it might have been two, three days later, both men were found washed up and lying stark naked on a beautiful beach frozen rock-solid, for winter arrives on Reindeer Lake in mid-October. That was Mother Nature at her most heartless.

Next, if time in Greek mythology plays second fiddle to space in the great scheme of things, then the distance or gap between that time and that space, in Indigenous mythology, is of even greater width, even greater breadth; in fact, that gap is one huge chasm that is all but unbridgeable — the same case, only in reverse, that exists in the sphere of Christian mythology. If time lords it over space with complete power in Christian mythology, then space lords it over time with complete power in Indigenous mythology. If time, in Christian mythology, is conceived of as one straight line, an arrow that travels with speed accelerating from point A to B to C, and ends there abruptly, then time, in Indigenous mythology, is one vast circle. And within that circle, within that womb, to give the notion some visceral perspective, lies the vast expanse of space, the vast expanse of land, the vast expanse of ocean, the vast expanse of air, the vast expanse of sunlight, of lake — up here in Canada, of lakes unlimited, of forests unlimited, of wildlife unlimited, of a garden of pleasure, a garden of joy unlimited, and of beauty unlimited and most, most wondrous.

And on that circle there is no beginning, there is no middle, and, most significantly, there is no end. Existence in the universe is merely one endless circle of birth and life and death and rebirth and life and death and rebirth so that those who lived in ages before us — our mothers, our grandmothers, our great-great-grandmothers, our children who have died, our loved ones — they live here with us, still, today, in the very air we breathe, in the shimmer of a leaf on that maple tree, in that shaft of sunlight that drifts in through your kitchen window and lands on your wrist, in your very skin (your mother's), in your very blood (your father's), in your very voice (your sister's, your aunt's). They are here. Tears of sorrow are to be shed, yes, but so are tears of joy, of rampant celebration.

Last comes the notion of paradise, of the Garden of Eden. In Indigenous mythology, there is no such tale, no such narrative — of eviction from what, in effect, is the human body, until the day we die — just as there is none in its Greek counterpart. According to that narrative, the way that dream world, that collective subconscious, is structured, we are *still* in that garden. At the very least, the Greeks were honest about the biological reality, both divine and human, of the singular act of sex, of the passing from one body to another of a certain essential fluid — blood, sweat, and tears are the very least of the great design — and of rampant, electrical, physical pleasure. Many parts of the world may be parched, treeless deserts — cursed by drought, by human error such as damming, by increasingly omnivorous raging wildfires, by floods, by an angry male god who has never had sex, but Canada, our home and native land, is *not*. Rather, she is the most spectacularly beautiful country on Earth, certainly the most water-wealthy, with one million freshwater lakes, most untouched as yet by radioactivity; my corner of Manitoba alone — that is, its northwesternmost extremity — has ten thousand lakes. Our garden is not a curse from an angry male god but rather a gift from a benevolent female god. And the great tree of knowledge? Well, in Christian mythology, we as a species are not to partake of the fruit of that tree. Only God has that right. In Greek and Indigenous mythologies, by contrast, that's why it's there, right there in the middle of the garden — that is, the human body — for us to partake of, for us to enjoy, for us to celebrate day in and day out.

Science, in all its brilliance — from quantum physics to cellular biology — has never been able to explain where the impulse of that first cell in the universe came from. And neither has religion, in all its incredible complexity, been able to explain, adequately, just where the life force of the common human being originates, where the movement inside that first cell inside the human body comes from. A new language, therefore, had to be invented — by the visionaries, the priests, the shamans of our respective societies — to articulate that origin. And that language is mythology.

Mythology, the exact halfway point between science and religion, that most elaborate of all fictions. Achi-thoogee-win, the exact halfway point between aachi-moowin and kithaas-kiwin. The language needed to describe a dream world where exist, where thrive, men with wings, horses with wings; where creatures half-human and half-god walk the Earth, just like the god Pan, or Weesaageechaak, the great Cree Trickster; where snakes talk to women (but not, for some reason, to men), women give birth without having had sex, dead men rise from the grave. And women — and men, too, like my dear friend Billy Boy Cut Throat — are, at one and the same time, both human and divine.

THREE

On Humour

RECITE THIS PARAGRAPH in front of a mirror and see what happens, first to your lips, then to your eyes, then to your cheeks, then to your nostrils, then to your face, and last to your shoulders. I'll bet you anything that not much happens. Nothing accelerates, nothing decelerates, not your breathing, not your pulse. All hang listless, as expressionless as lint on an old man's coat. There is not much humour built into the sentences, so why laugh lustily? Why even chuckle?

Now say these Cree words that follow in front of a mirror and see what happens, first to your lips, then to your eyes, then to your cheeks, then to your nostrils, then to your face, and then to your shoulders. You don't even have to look in a mirror to detect the adjustments that will transpire.

"Choochoos." And leave it there; don't move a muscle. The nickname of a man in old Brochet, it means "nipples." Say it again. "Choochoos." And freeze. See how your lips are already pointing in a manner slightly unseemly? Those speaking English would call it naughty, but we don't; to us, everything in life is naughty, comical, and moochigan (fun). At the sound of the syllables in the English language — nipples — the angel with the sword is unsheathing his weapon; you're cringing already. But see how your eyes are already giving off a Tricksterish twinkle? As if you are about to pinch Choochoos, the old man I speak of? And your cheek muscles have already tightened to the point where, like a band of elastic, they might well snap with a cartoon twang; your nostrils have narrowed to the point where your nose has lengthened by a tenth of an inch; your face is just one muscle twitch away from exploding with a gush that announces laughter; your shoulders are shaking, the bottom of your throat already revving up for a major event orgasmic in nature, life-changing in thrust.

Now try these words in that mirror — or to your

lover or, at the very least, to your best friend — and
see how the aforementioned parts of your face and
your body react to the syllables and even to the letters. Moomoos, which means bogeyman. Then this
one: pooseessss, which means pussy, our word for
cat — hey, that's how we heard the Moony-ass call
the furry little critter when they first brought one
to old Brochet. The first time we saw one, it was not
only an anomaly, it was evil incarnate. Some whis-
pered that it was complicit in Satan's necromancy,
so Mom reviled it; all she had to do was see its
tail and her spine shuddered. Which was why she
added three s's at the end of its name; not only did
she sound like she was hissing at the creature, but
the "sacred" letter also protected her, she insisted,
from possible expulsion to machee-skooteek (the
bad fire, our word for hell).

Now try chipoo-cheech (puppy). Tootoo-saap'wi
(tit water, our word for milk). Tootoo-simi-yaapi
(tit string, our word for bra). Egee-weepin-toochik
(which means they separated, or divorced, but literally means "they threw each other away," the
implication being "into the garbage"). Eegee-
cheestaa-skwaateet; the word is based on the verb
"cheestow," which means "pierce him" (as with a
fork), so eegee-cheestaa-skwaateet ends up meaning

"he got pierced with a fork to his death," which is
what happened to poor Jeesoos (our pronunciation
of the name Jesus) when he was crucified, for neither "crucified" nor "crucifixion" exists as a word in
Cree. And here's the doozy: eegee-paask'si-geepa-
thit. Pask'sigan means "gun," so the long word just
cited means "he went off like a gun," which is our
way of saying, "He had an orgasm." In English, you
choke with shame when you experience this word,
then, by way of penance, plunge into a litany of
doleful *"mea culpas"* and, if you're Catholic, ten Hail
Marys said giddyap fast. But in Cree, you scream.
You thrash and twist and writhe and churn. Every
single syllable of this Algonquian language pops
and sizzles with madcap energy, with sexual innu-
endo, which is why it laughs. And laughs so hard.

Even children use at liberty words such as
k'seet-noo ootas-neema — old man's balls, our word
for prunes, because that's what the wrinkled fruit
looked like to us when we first saw them. Oochees-
sak (maggots) was our word for rice, because that's
what the grain looked like to us when we first saw
it. Even ordinary terms like those for iron (for
pressing clothes, soosk-waygan, that which slides)
or ketchup (aspaa-chigan, that which goes on top)
or canned fruit (kaagoo-cheeg'wow, those that

(66)

float) cause gales of laughter. When was the last time the mention in English of ketchup or canned peaches made you double over in hysterics? Last, try something as dangerous as chastity belt; I'll write it in Cree but leave the English translation to your imagination — ana pagwaa-tee-oon ithi-gook kaaseech-skawat maw kagee-mati-ga-win. Ask a Cree friend to translate it for you and you will die and go up to heaven!

Welcome to pleasure; welcome to fun. Welcome to the Trickster and his sense of humour. Welcome to our world of rampant insanity. Kwayas kamoo-chigee-taanaa-wow. (Boy, are you going to have one good time.)

THE WORLD CAME ABOUT, AT LEAST IN CREE, as the result of the efforts of a female force of energy called Oomaa-maa, which translates roughly to the Great Mother, a miraculous entity that eventually came to be known in English as Mother Earth. And she, without acknowledgement of male contribution to the act of conception, gave birth first to the Thunderbird, who would protect the other creatures from the mysterious and destructive sea serpent Kinee-pick. The thunderbirds live in nests high in the mountains toward the setting sun, or so it is said. Clouds turn black and roll across the sky when the thunderbirds are angry or are fighting with Kinee-pick. Often when it rains and fire flashes from the sky, the voices of the thunderbirds cry out in anger. In Cree, we call them "oogi-toowak," which means "they who talk," similar to Christian and classical mythology, in which a male god talks while brandishing a thunderbolt. We humans are worms compared to the thunderbirds, who came into the world long before human beings were even a glimmer in the eyes of the goddess, that is, our dear Mother Earth.

The second creature to come from the womb of Oomaa-maa was Oma-ka-ki, the lowly frog, who was given sorcerers' powers to help control the insects of the world. The other animals often call upon Oma-ka-ki to help them when they are in trouble.

And third born was the clown called, in Cree, Weesaa-geechaak, and in English — the Trickster. Oomaa-maa gave Weesaa-geechaak many magical powers, among which was the ability to change himself into any shape he chose, especially when he had to save himself from danger. He was also an adventurer who liked to make mischief and play tricks on people, only to get himself hopelessly entangled in his own web of trouble. Sometimes he gets our people very angry. If you ever meet him, the Elders say, offer him some tobacco and he may help you. Tobacco is one of the four sacred herbs, the others being sage, cedar, and sweetgrass.

Oomaa-maa's fourth child was Ma-hee-gan, the wolf. Because Ma-hee-gan is the little brother of Weesaa-geechaak, they often travel together in the forest, having adventures. Weesaa-geechaak will sometimes turn himself into a little person and ride on the hairy back of his four-legged brother. Called the maymay-g'waysi-wak in Cree and its sister language Ojibway, these are little magic people, not unlike the Irish leprechaun, who live in low-lying bushes in the forest. Visible to humans only when they are in the throes of a vision induced by hunger, exhaustion, or some other crisis, they whisper and giggle at the folly of humankind. The rustle of leaves and low bushes in the breeze are their voices. In the olden days, before the arrival of electricity or motorized traffic or the Moony-ass, nature talked and people heard her and vice versa. Next came Amisk, the beaver. Amisk is greatly respected by our people. It is even said that the beavers were once humans in a different

world, but evil befell them and they became animals. Whenever you kill a beaver, say the Elders,
you must throw his bones back into the pond as
an offering to the spirit of the animal. Then fish,
rock, grass, trees, and the other animals eventually
emerged from the womb of Oomaa-maa. And for
eons, only they and the spirits inhabited the planet
because Weesaa-geechaak, the Trickster, had not
yet invented the beast called human.

Where the Elders, the priests, and the shamans
of Greek, Christian, and Indigenous mythologies —
that is, the mythologies' inventors — got these
stories is beyond the reach of human comprehen-
sion. Who was there, for example, to hear the King
of the Sky intone the immortal line "Let there be
light"? By the same token, who was there to hear
a red-nosed clown cackle, "Let there be laughter,"
thus kicking life into the universe?

HERE'S JUST ONE OF many, many Trickster stories.

Then came a period when the waters of the lakes
and the rivers began to rise and cover the forests.
Many of the animals drowned. The birds and the
animals were afraid that they had angered Oomaa-
maa. Some creatures said that the Mishi-pizhiw

(Great Animals) were digging in the bottom of a great lake and had opened the core of the world, which was full of water, causing Oomaa-maa to bleed to her death.

At last, only a small island remained with some birds and animals on it. But Weesaa-geechaak was on the island and he helped the animals build a great canoe. Beavers cut down the trees, and musk-rats tied the poles together with roots, while the frogs packed mud between the poles to make the great vessel float. The birds built a huge nest in the canoe so everyone would be warm and com-fortable, and Weesaa-geechaak built a roof over it. It rained and the waters kept rising until the great brown canoe floated off on the ocean. The animals and Weesaa-geechaak rode the big canoe for many years over stormy seas and through strong winds.

Finally, one day, the rain stopped and the great canoe rocked gently once more as the winds stopped blowing. Weesaa-geechaak realized to his horror that he had forgotten to bring along a piece of the earth with which to re-create a new world. The only way to obtain it was to get someone to dive to the bottom of the ocean; therefore, he tied a vine to Kitchi-amisk, a giant beaver, and told him to dive into the depths for some clay. After some time had passed, Weesaa-geechaak pulled the limp body of Kitchi-amisk up into the great boat. To his disappointment, there was no clay. Next he told Nin-gig, the otter, to dive for clay, but the same thing happened. The otter couldn't find the bottom and died.

In a last attempt, Weesaa-geechaak sent Wachask, the muskrat, into the ocean. The vine went down and down. When he finally pulled the muskrat up, he discovered that Wachask had drowned, but in his tiny paws lay a piece of clay. Weesaa-geechaak was so excited that he immediately brought the three swimmers back to life. He then put the clay in a pot and boiled it. The clay expanded over the sides of the pot, falling into the great sea until the land was reformed.

The next day, Weesaa-geechaak asked Geen-go-hongay, the wolverine, to travel around the Earth to find out how big it was. Geesis, the day sun, had not been in the sky twice before Geen-go-hongay returned.

"The Earth is not big enough yet," said Weesaa-geechaak to all the animals. He boiled the pot again and more clay fell into the ocean. Again, Geen-go-hongay journeyed around the world. The second time, he returned puffing and tired, but Weesaa-geechaak was still not satisfied with his work. He boiled the clay pot for the third time, and then he sent off the wolverine to measure his work.

Geen-go-hongay never returned. The world was big enough.

This is far from the only story that intersects with Christian and other world mythologies.

Meaning to say that it was the Trickster — not a man named Noah but a madcap clown — who re-created the world after the flood. With the help of the animals. But here's a story of the Trickster creating the season called pipoon (winter).

It was not long after the world had been reformed and Weesaa-geechaak was meeting with all the animals of the Earth to decide how long the snow should fall in the forests.

"How many moons should the winter have?" he asked the creatures.

A large bull moose with a great spread of horns replied, "There should be as many moons of winter as there are hairs on my body."

There was an immediate reaction from the rest of the animals. Some called the moose stupid, and others just shook their heads in disbelief. Weesaa-geechaak replied, "Surely there would be snow and coldness for a long time if I accepted your suggestion."

Amisk, the beaver, was the next to speak. "There should be as many moons of winter as there are scales on my tail."

Weesaa-geechaak stated that this would still make the winter quite long, and it would be hard for some of the animals to survive.

The lowly frog, Oma-ka-ki, squeaked, "There should be only as many moons as I have toes."

All of the beasts told him to be quiet because Oma-ka-ki was such a small creature. But Weesaa-geechaak decided that this would be a reasonable length for winter; hence, it came about that the winter of the Cree and Ojibway lasts five moons, the months of November, December, January, February, and March, the number of toes on Oma-ka-ki's foot.

Trickster exists in every single Indigenous Nation, and every single Indigenous language, from one end of the North American continent to the other. It all depends on the area and with it the Nation — what the politically incorrect used to call the "tribe." Whether that Nation be Cree or Blackfoot or Anishinaabe or Mi'kmaq or Haida or Innu, it has a Trickster in some form or other. The stories are interchangeable. Then again, all Tricksters are interchangeable. Or universal.

The next incarnation comes from the Anishinaabe Nation, what the politically incorrect used to call the Ojibway. The name of this Trickster is variously spelled as Nanabush or Nanabozho. And because the traditional territory of these people mostly surrounds the five Great Lakes, this story takes place on the largest of them all, what is known today as Lake Superior.

"Grandson," said Nanabozho's grandmother, his nokomis, one summer morning, "my hair is falling out because I have no oil to preserve it."

"Grandmother," said Nanabozho, "where can I get this oil?"

"You must go to the great lake in the north. This lake is the home of Meshena-Magwai, the giant sturgeon, the Great Chief of All Fish. Go and kill him. Bring him to me. Then we will boil enough oil out of him to last us to the end of time."

"Grandmother," said Nanabozho, "you must make the fish line and the fish hook. I will make the canoe."

Nanabozho then went to a lonely place on top of a hill. There he stayed for four days and four nights, fasting and praying to Gitche Manitou, the Everywhere Spirit, to bless his enterprise with success. Then he made his canoe out of birchbark.

He made the paddle from oak. It took a whole big oak tree to make it. His nokomis gave him the fish line and the fish hook. Then Nanabozho set out on the river that led to the Great Lake. He paddled out to its middle and threw out the line and the baited hook. In a loud voice, Nanabozho called out, "Meshena-Magwai, Chief of All Fish, take my hook."

Away down at the bottom of the lake, the Chief of All Fish heard him. He told Trout, "Swim up and see who it is who dares to call me in this manner."

Up on the surface, Nanabozho felt someone immensely strong tugging on his line. "It must be Meshena-Magwai," he thought, "the Chief of All Fish. No one else could do such tugging."

Trout had taken the bait. He pulled at the line with such force that Nanabozho's canoe was pulled halfway down to the bottom of the lake, standing upright. But Nanabozho was stronger than Trout. He managed to drag him into his boat. He looked at Trout and said, "You ugly, puny thing. You are not the Chief of All Fish. I think Meshena-Magwai is afraid to come up and fight me."

Trout was angry to be called ugly and puny. He jumped out of the boat, dove down to the bottom of the Great Lake, and told the Chief of All Fish, "It is Nanabozho who is up there. He has no manners. He called me bad names. He says you are afraid to come up and face him."

"Is that so?" said the Great Chief of All Fish. He called the great pike. "Nephew, go up there and teach Nanabozho some manners." Giant Pike swam to the surface, where he heard Nanabozho shouting, "Meshena-Magwai, Chief of All Fish, come and take my bait!"

In his boat, Nanabozho felt a tugging at his line. The pull was so strong that it made the canoe swirl around in circles again and again. It made the whole Great Lake foam and swirl and writhe and churn. The water rushed about Nanabozho's canoe in dizzying circles, making it spin wildly on its own axis. The waves formed an eddy that almost sucked Nanabozho and his canoe down to the lake bottom. But Nanabozho was mighty above all others. He succeeded in pulling Giant Pike into his canoe, though it took all his enormous strength. When Nanabozho saw what he had caught, he was disgusted.

"You insignificant, slimy thing!" he shouted. "You are not the Great Chief of All Fish. Is Meshena-Magwai trembling in fear of me? Is that the reason he does not dare come up to face me?"

With a mighty heave, Nanabozho flung Giant Pike back into the water.

Giant Pike at once dove straight down to the bottom of the lake to tell the Chief of All Fish, "Nanabozho says that you, oh Great Chief of All Fish, are afraid of him. He insulted me, calling me slimy and insignificant. Will you let him get away with this?"

"I guess I must take care of this matter myself," said the Great Chief of All Fish, and he began slowly to rise to the surface.

Away up above, Nanabozho was shouting, "Great Chief of All Fish, take my bait!"

Meshena-Magwai broke the surface, creating a huge wave that made the lake overflow in all directions, covering the whole country with man-high water. He made the waters boil. The Great Chief of All Fish was so big that no word could describe his size. With one great gulp, Meshena-Magwai swallowed up Nanabozho — canoe, paddle, and all.

Inside Meshena-Magwai's body, it was dark. Nanabozho heard a loud, reverberating *thump, thump, thump*. It echoed from the walls, which were the lining of Meshena-Magwai's stomach. Every thump shook his body like an earthquake. Nanabozho went rigid with fear. He quickly discovered that this great thumping sound came from the heart of the Great Chief of All Fish. Nanabozho never went anywhere without the war club dangling from his belt. He took the club and used it to beat the giant heart. After a while, the heartbeat got weaker and weaker. At last, it stopped altogether. Meshena-Magwai, the Great Chief of All Fish, was dead. The waves carried Meshena-Magwai's body to the shore. And there it lay in the sand.

Nanabozho had won his battle, but Meshena-Magwai's mouth was clamped shut. Nanabozho found himself trapped in the Great Chief of All Fish's body. What was he to do? "Maybe I will die in here," said Nanabozho. "Maybe I will die of starvation." But then he heard a faint gnawing sound. It came from a squirrel who was trying to make a hole through the Chief of All Fish's side. Nanabozho did not know how Squirrel had gotten inside the Fish Chief's body. It turned out that Squirrel was not strong enough to bore through to the outside.

Then Nanabozho shouted loudly, so loud that it made the whole Earth tremble, "This is Nanabozho calling from inside the Fish Chief's body. If there is a friend of mine outside, let him help me to get out."

There was a scratching sound on Meshena-Magwai's skin. It grew louder and louder. The squirrel continued to gnaw from the inside of the Great Chief of All Fish. From the outside, someone was trying to scratch his way in. Finally, the squirrel's teeth met the claws of a seagull. They had made a hole in the Great Chief of All Fish's side. Squirrel and Seagull widened the hole until it was big enough to let Nanabozho squeeze through with his canoe. For their help, he gave his two rescuers honouring names. He named Squirrel "Little Mighty Gnawer" and Seagull "Winged Mighty Scratcher."

Nanabozho took leave of his two helpers. He tied the body of the Great Chief of All Fish to his canoe and paddled upriver to the home of Nokomis. He and Nokomis cut up Meshena-Magwai's body and boiled it down to oil. They got so much that it formed a whole lake of oil, enough to treat the hair of all women to the end of time.

At one point in my career, I adapted this story to an opera commissioned by the Montreal Symphony Orchestra, except I spliced it with the biblical story of Jonah and the Whale. Audiences saw and understood the parallels: Jonah was Nanabozho, and the whale was God — that is, the monotheistic Christian God. But what is the difference between the two stories? Nanabozho is funny; he is a clown.

Jonah is not, the Christian God even less so. And the arguments the Trickster has with God from inside his belly are hysterical, bordering on violent — one way or another, he wants out of this trap. At one juncture, in his frustration, the Trickster singes the deity's heart with a torch he has produced out of nowhere — hey, he's a magician, he can make fire at the snap of a finger — and yells at him, "Why are you so unfunny? Where's your sense of humour? Don't you know how to laugh, you joyless jerk?" The torch having found its mark, the whale starts thrashing and twisting and writhing and churning from the pain in his heart, in the process kicking off a storm that threatens to inundate the entire planet. This is one example of the god from the monotheistic dream world going head to head with the all-encompassing force of divinity from the pantheistic dream world. And the whole world feels the impending deluge. Will the planet laugh? Or will it not?

Because there exists but one god in monotheism, it naturally follows that there exists but one superhero in that collective subconscious. Offspring of the one god in that system and a mortal woman named Mary, thus making him another half-god/half-mortal, he displayed legendary feats of courage. His life story is so well known the whole world over because yet one more definition of mythology is a story that your intellect is incapable of believing but your spirit does with every single ounce of its being. That story is so powerful that an entire civilization has been built upon its bedrock, an entire planet given shape and substance by it.

Still, not once in the entire life story of this hero have I ever heard him laugh. A thousand pages of biographical detail, depending on the edition and the language, have I read, but I have yet to hear him chuckle, guffaw, or chortle. Kind, intelligent, wise beyond his youthful years, courageous, capable of miracles unheard of in the history of the human race, and capable, moreover, of suffering beyond all human suffering, but one thing he wasn't — a barrel of laughs. Which is where he comes to a parting of ways with the Indigenous superhero.

Our Trickster is zany. He is crazy. Psychedelic. He is explosive, maniacal, unpredictable, disruptive, irascible, profane, scatological, contrary. He is insane, ridiculous, funny, hysterical, cowardly, clumsy, dishonest, deceitful, self-serving, arrogant, the ultimate over-the-top madcap fool. Strictly speaking, he has no shape, no physical dimension, not as human, not as animal; he was, that is to say, never anthropomorphized by the people who pay him homage. Not until the late twentieth century, with the emergence of the first generation of modern Indigenous artists like Norval Morrisseau and the late dancer and choreographer René Highway, did this start happening. If the Trickster was, until then, merely a spark or a flash of electrical energy that made nerves twitch or dreams time travel, then now he was, suddenly, a dash of paint faintly resembling a young man running. Or, in the case of the theatre, jumping or dancing or floating over the highest skyscrapers in Canada in a figure reminiscent of Billy Boy Cut Throat.

Figures from the sphere of polytheistic thought still resonate in his striking presence. Hermes, the Trickster god, also known as the messenger god who escorts souls to the land of the dead — and who is the son of Zeus and a nymph of the Pleiades named Maia — is his closest facsimile. But his persona is also decipherable in the figure of Dionysus, the god of wine, of cannabis-and-wine-induced insane celebrations in hotel rooms in downtown Toronto. Then there is Pan: half-goat/half-man, pleasure-loving sybarite, and resident of the garden of pleasure, a creature of the soil if ever there was one. And there is Priapus, the ultimate sex god. Even the love goddess Aphrodite holds her place in our great clown's soul, if only in the person of her bi-gendered progeny (with her brother, Hermes), Hermaphrodite.

All the cultures in the world have Tricksters, from fools and court jesters in medieval European courts to Lords of Misrule at English Christmas festivities of times long past — Abbots of Unreason in Scotland — to Pierrot and Harlequin in Italy's commedia dell'arte to Shakespeare's Puck and Touchstone and Feste and King Lear's fool and, for that matter, America's Charlie Chaplin, Buster Keaton, Red Skelton, Laurel and Hardy, Abbott and Costello, the Three Stooges, Lucille Ball, Carol Burnett, Lily Tomlin, Phyllis Diller, cartoon characters like Bugs Bunny and Mickey Mouse and Wile E. Coyote. They are here and have always been here to remind us that if we don't laugh, we will die. Like the Native Trickster — and especially like the Native Trickster — they are here to remind us that the reason for existence on planet Earth is not to suffer, not to wallow in guilt, not to apologize for a crime we did not commit, but to have one blast of a time, to laugh ourselves to death.

For example, here is Iktomi, the Trickster of the

Lakota Nation (formerly known as Sioux) of South
Dakota. He belongs, as well, to related branches
of this same Nation; Dakota is just one, Oglala
another. In the traditional stories, he appears as
half-man and half-spider, a very foolish, hard-to-
pin-down shape-shifter.

Iktomi was sitting on a log one fine morning
sunning himself when he saw Cetan, the Hawk,
flying about.

"Brother," cried Iktomi, "give me a ride."

The good-natured Hawk let Iktomi climb on his
back. Once he was up in the air, Iktomi enjoyed
the flight and the fine view, but soon he was bored.
Iktomi is always bored, unless he can play a joke on
someone. He decided to have some fun at Hawk's
expense.

Whenever they encountered another creature — an eagle, buzzard, or magpie — Iktomi made
a gesture indicating that Hawk was a stupid, no-
account good-for-nothing. Thus, he played Hawk
for a fool. He thought Hawk could not see him
doing that. He thought, "Hawks don't have eyes
on the backs of their heads."

What Iktomi forgot was that Hawk could see
their shadow on the ground and could watch Iktomi
making fun of him.

"I'll get even with that tricky Spider-Man," thought Hawk, and he suddenly turned over, now flying upside down.

Iktomi lost his grip and fell through the air, landing inside a hollow tree. He was still trying to find his way out of the tree when it began to rain. It rained very hard. The tree was very dry. It soaked up the water like a sponge and swelled up. Poor Iktomi was being crushed to his death. In his pain and fear, he began to pray.

"Great Spirit, why did you make me so smart that I always try to fool everybody? In the end, I am only fooling myself. Please save me! Have pity on me!" Thus, Iktomi humbled himself. His former pride and wickedness made him feel very small, so small that he was able to crawl out of that tree. Sometimes a little humility and prayer can be a good thing.

This is just one of innumerable stories of the Trickster from all the Native Nations across North America, stories as old as time, that speak of his adventures stealing the sun, stealing the summer, inventing fire, ad infinitum . . . But central to the mythmaking process is the interaction between the various levels of life involved in the narrative, what would be considered the "what" of the matter. In the polytheistic and monotheistic superstructures, there are but two of these levels: the level of divinity and the level of humanity. In the pantheistic model, however, there is a third: the level of nature. And key to the narrative drive of each of these three superstructures — the "why" of the matter, if you will — is the manner in which one level intermingles with the other, thus changing that level or being changed by it. Some of these interminglings are accomplished through overt encounters involving sex — involving biology, it might be said — some through visions that amount to illusions optical or otherwise — daydreams, for instance — and some through actual nocturnal dreams. They have to meet and intermingle or our story would have no substance, would not be worth telling. Indeed, this meeting of minds, so to speak, is what makes the universal stories so exciting, so filled with drama, so colourful, and so powerful. Without that dimension, life on Earth is left an experience bereft of colour, pedestrian, boring, not worth living. In this way, life on Earth is imbued with magic.

In the polytheistic universe, we have seen snippets of the manner in which the various gods and goddesses interact one with the other, frequently engendering, in the process, another generation of gods and goddesses. However, it is the interactions between gods and mortals, not gods and gods, that concerns us, because it is from these encounters that a new breed of being is born, one who is half-god and half-mortal, from whence comes the classical definition of the term "hero." In just such a manner is humankind elevated to a status divine, otherworldly, even eternal.

In the polytheistic collective subconscious, Zeus, the King of the Sky, is responsible for many examples of such interactions. To sate his limitless concupiscence, he would look down at the earth with a wandering eye and see attractive mortals gambolling about in the garden of Arcadia and ravish them (again, a euphemism for rape). The upshot of these encounters was the conception of beings that were both god and mortal at the same time, meaning they fit neatly into the classical definition of hero. Besides his adventure with Leda, the princess of Sparta, another well-known Zeus dalliance was with Danae, a mortal woman and princess of Argos, a city state just north of Sparta. When her father, the King of Argos, heard a prophesy that a son of his daughter would one day kill him, he imprisoned her in a subterranean chamber with a roof that was open to the sky, the opening through which, disguised as, of all things, a shower of gold, unstoppable Zeus was able to gain access to the star-crossed princess. The result? The birth of the hero Perseus, whose foremost claim to fame was the beheading with a sword of the snake-haired Gorgon Medusa, from which wound sprang the winged horse Pegasus. Imagine a world where a horse has wings, where a woman has coiling snakes for hair and eyes so deadly they turn onlookers to rock!

The most famous result of a Zeus dalliance was classical mythology's greatest hero, a man/god named Hercules, famed for his courage and feats of strength; slaying the many-headed sea monster, the Hydra, was only one in a long line of his exploits.

Still, impressive as they are, not one of these heroes was known for his laughter, his sense of humour. Except perhaps for Odysseus, grandson of the mischievous messenger god Hermes and legendary hero known for his cunning intellect. But overall, it would be difficult to see polytheism as a dream world full of gods who laugh.

By sharp contrast, this is what we do with the Native Trickster figure in our theatre...

Away out in a place unspecified, Trickster comes upon two coyotes preparing to have lunch. As he is hungry, as he always is, he insinuates himself into their company so he can eat some of their food. Weesaa-geechaack was always insinuating himself into people's company so he could get something out of them. In fact, there is a verb based on his name — ee-weesaa-geechaa-googaa-soot (Cree words can be very long), which means "to ingratiate oneself" or "to pretend to be" or even "to snivel" (in the act of pretending to be) or even, and more colloquially, "to kiss ass," though, to be more literal, it means "to be like Weesaa-geechaak."

But to get back to the two coyotes eating lunch, as there is only so much food to go around, they don't want Weesaa-geechaak there. Offended, Trickster walks off to come up with an idea to trick them into letting him join them. He comes back. As it turns out, there are two trees standing some two metres behind the banquet table. Two things are to be noted about these trees. First, they are birch, so they are pliable; they bend easily. Second, they share a root, so, like conjoined twins, they are connected at the base. They stand leaning outward so that, together, they look like a tall V, without leaves, as the season is spring.

"Cousins, cousins," says Trickster, all syrupy sweet.

"Yes?" say the coyotes as they, lips all greasy,

chew on the drumstick of a juicy young ptarmigan, a subarctic wild chicken that is very tasty, especially when roasted on an open fire.

"Please give me some meat," says Trickster.

"We have a surprise for you over there," says one coyote to the unwanted visitor. To lure him away from the food, the coyotes indicate the birch trees that stand V-shaped two metres behind them.

"You do?" says Trickster.

"We do," confirm the coyotes, then continue, "it's hidden in the crotch of those two trees over there. All you have to do is reach in and you will find a box."

Then as Weesaa-geechaak turns his back to walk to the trees with his mouth watering, the coyotes scoot off on tiptoe. Weesaa-geechaak kneels at the foot of the pair of trees and roots around with one hand, looking for his "gift." Eventually, he is rooting around with such violence that he causes the trees to start swaying. The two coyotes have made their way behind the trees, where they are squatting, invisible to Weesaa-geechaak, and manoeuvring the trees so that they are swaying, all as they, the coyotes, moan, "Ohhhhhh, ohhhhh, ohhhhh," as if in great pain (or great pleasure, depending on your taste or state of mind). Meanwhile,

Weesaa-geechaak is rooting around with increasing effort and urging, "Come on, box, I know you're in there. Come on, box, I know you're in there." So violent have the Trickster's efforts become that the trees are now moaning, "It hurts, it hurts, ohhhhh, ohhhhh, ohhhhh…"

Suddenly, the two coyotes let go of their respective trees. *Snap!* And Trickster is caught in the trap. He yowls, "Ayeeeeeeeeee!!!" as the coyotes calmly return to their meal.

When we produced this story as a play, we did it as a school show, and by the time the trees were moaning, "It hurts, it hurts," the children were screaming with glee. But the teachers were horrified. Why? Because the two leafless trees looked like a woman's naked legs held up in the air and opening and closing and opening and closing, all while the "woman" is moaning with pleasure and Trickster is going, "Come on, box." This was utterly unintentional; regardless, this bit of theatrical tomfoolery got our little theatre company fired and the rest of our school tour cancelled. But that is a typical Trickster event. The cosmic clown gave us a kick in the pants for mocking him, and we lost our jobs!

In another show called *The Sage, the Dancer and the Fool*, I foolishly adapted James Joyce's gigantic

novel *Ulysses*, the story of one day in the life of a
man living in Dublin, which is based, in turn, on
Homer's Greek epic poem *The Odyssey*. The play
details one day in the life of a Cree man living in
the city of Toronto, except that it does it in tripli-
cate — that is, the three titular characters play one
person. The Sage represents the intellect of the
hero, the Dancer his spirit, and the Fool his body.
The three shift in and out of each other with gesture, movement, and language in Cree and English.
And when the latter takes the lead — that is, the
Fool — he is Weesaa-geechaak, the Cree Trickster.
This play was an early effort in the technique of
interweaving Greek mythology, Christian mythology, and North American Indigenous mythology.
One of my earliest plays, it was written in 1984.
This was a time of massive social change in Native
communities. Prior to 1960, Native people were
mostly relegated to reserves and rural settings,
mostly in the north and in the west. It wasn't until
they got the right to vote in federal elections in
March 1960 — at least in Canada — that they were
free, for the first time, to leave those reserves and
seek in urban centres employment, advanced edu-
cation, and liberty in general. When they arrived
in the cities, they had to make certain adjustments

to their lifestyle and thinking. For the first time in their lives, they had to change from circular thinking to straight-line thinking. And this was the adjustment — the voyage, as it were — that I tried to address with this play.

The hero as the Sage wakes up one morning and, awestruck, sees that all is a straight line: skyscrapers and cement, a far cry from the circle of nature at its most wondrous — caribou moss and forests of spruce and smoke from campfires — that he grew up with in Northern Manitoba. For the rest of the day, the hero-in-triplicate rides the storm that is the tension between these two ideas, paralleling, all along, the epic voyage of Ulysses and his encounters with all kinds of creatures and monsters. After working hard all morning at a government office near Toronto's upscale Yorkville neighbourhood, the Sage goes for lunch at a restaurant and there meets his cyclops, the Weetigo, the cannibal spirit of Cree myth, gorging himself on human flesh. The Dancer takes over here and does a spectacular Martha Graham–inspired modern dance with the monster, the six-metre-long tablecloth made of muslin trailing behind and swirling all around him like a shaft of wind moving in slow motion, the monster, a dummy made of cloth and stuffing, swinging from his neck by the arms as if he is eating him. The soundtrack is mastication and slurping and burping and even farting that grows from the emissions of just one person to two to ten to fifty to a hundred to a thousand, the volume increasing until it is unbearable. All while, sitting at one end of this very long table that hangs at a slant, the Sage plays gorgeous atmospheric cocktail piano and the Fool/Trickster, sitting at the other end of the table, recites an insane monologue about the consumerism in the city that is devouring the souls of entire societies. The effect was spectacular. By end, the Dancer — the hero's spirit — is dancing a beautiful ballet at the top of the tallest skyscraper in Canada, right there on Bay Street in downtown Toronto, the nation's financial heart. It was the first time in history that the spirit of the Native Trickster had ever been seen in an urban environment. At that point in our history, the collective spirit of Native people had made the transition from forest-dweller to urban phenomenon, a social reality that we see continue today, from one day to the next to the next. To get here, the Indigenous person is guided every step of the way by the central hero figure from our mythology.

Thus did Trickster theatre, art, and literature emerge into the world from the furthest reaches of our collective racial memory, as first a spark, then a glimmer, then a flame, then a raging fire, to guide us through thin and through thick, through crises such as illness, hunger — certain starvation when the Weetigo faced us square in the eye — mental disorders such as depression, paranoia, fear, terror — terror at the prospect of death, terror at the prospect of being exterminated as a race. A mythology still in its early stages of development in 1492 — a baby still taking its first and very tentative steps — it was interrupted and grossly subverted. If the marriage between the sky god Zeus and his wife, the Earth goddess, Hera, was violent, then it was nothing in comparison to the moment when the one Christian God met Mother Earth on these shores and the aggression was total — he almost killed her. But didn't. The culture could have disappeared. The figure of the Trickster could have disappeared forever. The culture came close to disappearing. The figure of the Trickster came close to disappearing. But it didn't. It hung on by a hair. And hung on and hung on and hung on, if by one spark. And that is the spark that Indigenous artists stoked to life. Not least of which did these Trickster stories they tell make us laugh, and laughter is medicine. In fact, never before has laughter saved an entire race of people in quite this manner.

A reason why these stories seem so simplistic — like children's stories or cute little folktales — is that they are being told in English, which is too serious, too intellectual a language for them. As well, so much of this "library" has been destroyed by the Church so all that is left is cinders, scraps of this and scraps of that, scraps that our artists have been picking up and piecing back together. These stories come to us from the mists of time, when magic was alive. A time when witchcraft flourished and magicians thrived; humans were shape-shifters who had the ability to transform into beings part human, part animal; dwarves, elves, and giants walked the land; tales existed of humans with wings, horses with wings, of people rising from the dead and living forever. Then again, which is more believable? A human with wings? A horse with wings? Or a clown god trapped in the belly of a whale who talks? Still, this is the clown who lives at the core of our imaginations, our dreams, our collective subconscious. We lived in the boreal forests of the Far North, and that forest was alive with magic. That land breathed; it talked. The relationship between humans, animals, and nature was real; it was intense. At a time when there was no postal system, no telephone, no electricity, no radio or television, and certainly no internet, what else were we to depend on than dreams for communicating with each other over some of the longest distances on Earth. Did you know, for instance, that the distance between the Manitoba–Nunavut border and the North Pole, which could be said to be almost in Canada, is the same as that between Vancouver and Halifax?

When the first generation of Native people emerged out of the forests of the Far North armed with university degrees and started picking up the pieces of a shattered culture, these "children's stories" that come to us from the furthest reaches of our collective racial memory were all we had to work with. That's all we artists had to hang on to, to build on. And we keep building, building, building. Egosi (so be it).

LAST, HERE'S A STORY ABOUT THE ROLE of Weesaageechaak, the Trickster's Cree incarnation, in the coming into being of tibikye-geesis, the "night sun," our word for the moon.

There are to this day a race of sky people living in the misty white clouds. Very little is known about these supernatural people because they are not often mentioned in our stories. But it is known that, in the very long ago, there was no moon; only geesis, the day sun, crossed the heavens. Geesis was kindled and kept burning by one of the sky men, who had a son and a daughter.

As the golden leaves fell from the birch trees season after season, the sky father became very old and weary of his duty, the kindling of the sun's fires. He told his children that one day he would disappear forever and they must look after the sun's fires; otherwise, the people of the world would die.

Finally, one day, the father returned to his wigwam high in the clouds and told the children that he had finished his obligations to the Great Spirit. No longer would he need the sun's fires, and he was leaving forever. The children were very sad that their father had left them. They talked of his goodness and his kind ways during the black of the night, but soon it was morning and time for the first of the geesis to be set alight.

"I will set geesis aflame," said the young girl.

"No, I am the man of this family now, and it

is my privilege and honour to look after the sun's flames," said the boy.

They could not agree, and soon they were fighting each other, rolling in the clouds, pulling one another's hair. The time to light the sun's fires came and passed; still, the young sky people quarrelled fiercely. Below on the Earth, people and animals stared into the black sky, waiting for geesis to send his warm light to them. They were frightened because they knew they could not live without the sun.

Weesaa-geechaak was travelling in the forest and he realized something was wrong. The sky people were not looking after the sun. Shape-shifting into the form of binay-sih (bird), he flew into the floating clouds to see what had happened. He found the children fighting. Angrily, he said, "Stupid children! Why are you fighting like starving wolves? Why are you not kindling the fires of geesis?"

"Our father has left us, great Weesaa-geechaak, and I am to care for geesis," the girl said quickly.

"And you quarrel and fight while there is blackness on the earth below? How foolish, sky children. You must be punished," Weesaa-geechaak told them bitterly.

Then the great Weesaa-geechaak told the sky children their fates. "You, sky man, shall tend the fires of geesis until the end of time. You, sky woman, will look after another eternal fire in the heavens. It will burn only in the darkness of the night and will be very difficult to keep aflame, so you will have to work hard to keep it from dying out. Never again will the two of you be together, but a few days of the year, you will cross the blueness together and be able to see each other, if from a distance."

And this is how tibikye-geesis came into the world. The night sun has guided many a lonely hunter through the dark forest, as it has us, the Indigenous artists, for it's been a dark and lonely road, a frightening one, filled with pitfalls that almost killed us, as, indeed, it did do to some of us. All the more reason, then, to bring on the clown, bring on the language, the stories that saved laughter for the pleasure of generations past, present, and future.

FOUR

On Sex and Gender

IN THE BEGINNING, THERE WERE only two human beings in this world: Old Man Coyote and Coyote Woman. Old Man Coyote lived on one side of the world, Coyote Woman on the other. By chance, they met.

"How strange," said Old Man Coyote. "We are exactly alike."

"I don't know about that," said Coyote Woman. "You're holding a bag. What's inside it?"

Old Man Coyote reached into his bag and brought out a penis. "This odd thing."

"It is indeed an odd thing," said Coyote Woman. "It looks funny. What is it for?"

"I don't know," said Old Man Coyote. "I don't know what to use it for. What do you have in *your* bag?"

Coyote Woman dug deep into her bag and came up with a vagina. "You see?" she said. "We are not alike. We carry different things in our bags. Where should we put them?"

"I think we should put them into our navels," said Old Man Coyote. "The navel seems to be a good place for them."

"No, I think not," said Coyote Woman. "I think we should stick them between our legs. That way they'll be out of the way."

"Well, all right," said Old Man Coyote. "Let's put them there."

They placed their things between their legs.

"You know," said Coyote Woman, "it seems to me that the strange thing you have there would fit this odd thing of mine."

"Well, you might be right," said Old Man Coyote. "Let's find out." He stuck his penis into Coyote Woman's vagina.

"Um, that feels good," said Coyote Woman.

"You are right," said Old Man Coyote. "It feels very good, indeed. I have never felt this way before."

"Neither have I," said Coyote Woman. "It occurred

to me that this might be the way to make other human beings. It would be nice to have company."

"It certainly would," said Old Man Coyote. "Just you and me would become boring."

"Well, in any case, doing what we just did should result in bringing forth more human beings. What should they be like?" said Coyote Woman.

"Well, I think they should have eyes and a mouth going up and down."

"No, no," said Coyote Woman. "Then they would not be able to see well and food would dribble out of the lower corners of their mouths. Let's have their eyes and their mouths go crosswise."

"I think the men should order the women about," said Old Man Coyote. "And the women should obey them."

"We'll see about that," said Coyote Woman. "I think the men should pretend to be in charge and the women should pretend to obey, but, in reality, it should be the other way around."

"I can't agree to this," said Old Man Coyote.

"Why quarrel?" said Coyote Woman. "Let's just wait and see how it will work out."

"All right, let's wait and see. How should the men live?"

"The men should hunt, kill buffalo and bears,

and bring the meat to the women. They should protect the women at all times."

"Well, that would be dangerous for the men,"
said Old Man Coyote. "A buffalo bull or a bear could
kill a man. Is it fair to put the men in such danger?
What should the women do in return?"

"Why, let the women do the work," said Coyote
Woman. "Let them cook, fetch water, and scrape
and tan hides with buffalo brains. Let them do
all these things while the men take a rest from
hunting."

"Well then, we agree upon everything," said Old
Man Coyote. "Then it's settled."

"Yes," said Coyote Woman. "Now why don't you
stick that funny thing of yours between my legs
again."

IN THE BEGINNING, THERE WERE only two human
beings in this world: Franklin Fox and Jane
Keegway. At least for each other they were the
world's only human beings, that's how deeply in
love they were, or thought they were, the night
they met. Franklin Fox lived on one side of the
village of Brochet, Manitoba, toward the head-
land that led southward with its now obsolescent

old cemetery whose tall wooden crucifix commanded the point as the only memorial left still standing. Jane Keegway lived at the far other end of the village, where a little river separated the northern and last kilometre from the rest. Just teenagers when they met, they locked glances at the northern end of the footbridge that crossed this river. At that point, tall and gangly Franklin Fox changed his mind and turned back south; he would walk with Jane Keegway toward the central part of the village, where was situated the new cemetery, the church, the one-room schoolhouse, and the southern half of the village in its bangly, jangly complexity. They walked; they talked. They talked about the weather, they talked about the land, they talked about the forest and the lake and the islands on Reindeer Lake — at the northern tip of which sits perched like a cherry old Brochet — of which there are hundreds, perhaps even thousands. They talked about the birds, they talked about the animals, they talked about the past, the present, and the future. Untold times that summer did they walk that trail, talking all along of life and love, the possibility of marriage, the possibility of children, of grandchildren, of great-grandchildren.

As it so happens, a field of tall wild grasses stood swaying in the breeze like widows lamenting, starting at about the halfway point between the south end of the village and the old cemetery in the distance and running all the way, going from west to east, from the low spruce forest that guarded the cabin of Ma Gloire Moorah and his wife, Misty Mary, and the lake, and through which wound mutely the sandy trail that constituted a part of the route traversed on a basis "alarmingly regular," according to the wives of Brochet village, by Franklin Fox and Jane Keegway. All through this area, the long and wide expansive field of tall wild grasses grew in summer to the height of grown-ups and so was ideal for children playing pickle-in-the-bun and hide-and-seek. And for lovers, legitimate or otherwise, to engage their bodies in the arduous contortions of making love. In fact, many is the time a young woman has been assaulted in just such a manner. The Dene girls, in particular, were highly susceptible to this sad situation at the hands of boys not Dene but Cree. The two Native Nations, radically different one from the other in language and ethnicity, shared the village, the latter more numerous, and therefore stronger, than the former. This was the case with Jane Keegway. Part

Cree and part Dene, she was vulnerable — in spite of the fact that her father, Paul Keegway, was the best dog sledder in all Brochet. Franklin Fox was Cree completely, and the lustful urges of young Cree men were known for their vigour, as they still are.

By the middle of the summer, Franklin Fox had fallen in love, or thought he had, with Jane Keegway, and Jane Keegway had fallen in love, or thought she had, with Franklin Fox. One August evening, when the moon was at its fullest and a breeze from Saskatchewan was making nature — the willows, the grasses, the raspberry bushes — sway like dancers, they paused for a spell at those tall grasses and nama-teed (disappeared). As if by a random act of wizardry, they were gone "for ten minutes, perhaps fifteen," said a witness, who also said that Jane Keegway was seen "after those minutes" weaving her way "stunned, as by a blow," away from that "garden" toward the lakeshore, with strands of grass and wild vegetation wound in her hair "as by Lagwa-choo" (the village hairdresser). Franklin Fox was seen walking away, likewise stunned, though not so much "as by a blow" but "as though drained" of a certain "mooskami" (a broth, as for soup), said this eyewitness, though going in the opposite direction, toward the rock-pocked forest of scraggly spruce in whose embrace lived Ma Gloire Moorah and his wife, Misty Mary.

She got pregnant (Jane Keegway, not Misty Mary). Whether or not she agreed to Franklin Fox's manly request for her hand in marriage some three months later, she had no choice. In those days, old Brochet was diehard Catholic, governed by the priest, Father Eemshaa-thik, with a fist made of iron. What he said from his pulpit on Sunday mornings terrified the people into submission. Babies born out of wedlock, said Father Eemshaa-thik, "are marked for life with the sign of Satan." From the day they were born, they were lepers, pariahs, personae non gratae. Which spelled the beginning of the end for Jane Keegway, she of the burnished complexion and almond ooskee-sigwa (eyes).

At sixteen, she married Franklin Fox. And over the course of the next two decades, they had children. And children and children. The first sign of trouble came when Franklin Fox was not yet twenty, when he told her she had given their first-born son a mark.

"What kind of mark?" asked Jane Keegway-now-Fox in all innocence.

"The mark of Satan," he answered grim-faced.

She let it pass. Hers was a personality that was

pliant, humble, and generous. But two years later, after the birth of their third child, he told her she was stupid. Five years later, he told her she was ugly. Twelve years later, after their tenth child, he told her she was by far "the worst damn mother" he had ever seen in all Brochet. Fights broke out, screaming matches, punches. The psychological, emotional, and physical abuse kept on mounting, while Jane Keegway kept giving birth to one child after another after another. "Contraception," boomed Father Eemshaa-thik from his pulpit one Sunday morning when Jane Keegway showed up wearing sunglasses to hide a black eye, "is Satan's way of enticing you women into the flames of suffering eternal." Eventually, Jane Keegway had fifteen children. Three of them were "not even Franklin's," went certain whispers that Franklin heard in unlikely places from unlikely sources. Still, the whispers were numerous and loud enough for Franklin Fox to believe them. His anger hardened.

Late one night in mid-September, Paul Keegway, Jane's now ageing father, a man much admired for his peaceful manner, was sitting at home with his wife, Aroozalee Keegway (Aroozalee is the Cree way of pronouncing Rosalie). In those days, old Brochet had no electricity, so they weren't watching television or even listening to a radio. They were just sitting there, quietly, in their living room, listening to the breathing of the great subarctic. Suddenly, they heard feet stomping on the little wooden steps that climbed to their back door. The door burst open, and there was Jane, their sixth daughter of ten. Her face had been reduced to the look and texture of raw ground beef by repeated hard contact with a length of firewood, her head swollen to twice its size. Her husband, Franklin, had beaten her, she told her parents upon their asking. Aroozalee Keegway rushed to the bathroom to vomit. And, throwing on his jacket and baseball cap, Paul Keegway walked out the door. As for Jane Keegway, she of the burnished complexion and almond eyes dropped to the couch and almost died.

It was midnight when Paul Keegway walked out of that house and half past twelve when he walked back in. The world's most loving and peaceful man, he had come "this close" to killing the man he knew, and had loved, as Franklin Fox, he of the craggy, long-limbed insouciance. One punch square in the jaw had he given the man whose eyes were red from alcohol consumption. And he was out, dead to the world. And Jane Keegway-now-Fox moved in with her parents, with fifteen children, ten of them her own, five of them her young grandchildren. But she went back to Franklin Fox just four months later.

"Divorce, separation," thundered Father Eemshaathik from his elevated perch at St. Pierre Church in old Brochet ten times that year, "neither is allowed by the Catholic Church."

IN THE BEGINNING, THERE WERE only two human beings in this world: Manfred Night and Rose Oohoo. At least for each other, they were the world's only human beings, that's how deeply in love they were, or thought they were, when they first met. Manfred Night lived on an island across from the village of old Brochet, a good kilometre directly across from the store called Companeek (our name for the Hudson's Bay Company, which ruled Brochet economically). The island was as pretty as a garland of flowers, no bigger than two large schoolyards, and held three log cabins that looked from a distance like stamps on letters. Rose Oohoo, meanwhile, lived in front of the old cemetery on the mainland, where her father was a fisherman whose nose for trout was the envy of the village — his catch was always the largest.

Manfred Night and Rose Oohoo met by chance at the counter at the Companeek store, where Rose and her sisters were buying lengths of cotton for the making of dresses, shirts, pants, whatever was needed, for, in those days, women made the clothing for their families. Then just sixteen, Rose Oohoo locked glances with Manfred Night, then eighteen, if only for a portion of one quick second. Which was enough for Manfred Night to make his move. With a twinkle in his eye, he casually addressed the winsome young woman: "You buying material for a wedding dress?"

Back then, white wedding dresses were unknown in the North; the nearest store that sold such items was in Winnipeg, some 1,300 kilometres to the south, at a time of limited travel — no roads, no cars, no airports. So a homemade dress was the only option, generally of floral-patterned cotton of the kind one found at the Companeek store. Rose Oohoo blushed pink and pretty at Manfred Night's words. At that juncture, Rose Oohoo's mother pulled her away, for she knew that the young man was fishing, and her feeling for the Nights was at best unpleasant, as she had said to her six daughters on more than one occasion. Secretly, however, Rose Oohoo's feelings for Manfred Night had already been awoken by the wayward glance of the man himself. A certain urge told her that she wanted marriage, that she wanted babies, that she wanted a family; he was a cad, she knew, but a handsome cad, one with a talent for the hunting life. Ducks, geese, ptarmigan, caribou, moose, rabbit — he would make a handsome provider, she was sure of it.

Manfred Night and Rose Oohoo started seeing each other, especially in the evenings, which, up north, in mid-August, are balmy and silken and go on forever. They were ready for a life of joy and fulfillment, Rose Oohoo was sure of it. So off toward the main part of the village, where lay proudly the new cemetery with its tombstones of granite, the church, and the one-room schoolhouse, would walk the couple when evening came and Rose Oohoo had done her duties at home as daughter.

By the middle of the summer, Rose Oohoo had fallen in love, truly, madly, and deeply, or thought she had, with Manfred Night. In fact, one August evening, when the moon was at its fullest and a breeze from Saskatchewan was making the verdure sway seductively, they paused for a spell of perhaps ten minutes at those tall grasses and disappeared as by an act of wizardry of the sort that the shaman Misti-goso was known for.

Rose Oohoo got pregnant, which spelled the beginning of the end for Rose Oohoo, she of the pale, soap-like complexion and limpid eyes. At age eighteen, she got married to Manfred Night. And over the course of the next two decades, they had children. And children and children.

One winter day, Molly Night, Holly Night, Velma Night, and Evangeline Night, all Rose Oohoo-now-Night's young daughters and all between the ages of six and twelve, came home from school at lunchtime, something they did of an ordinary day. Their brothers were absent, gone by bush plane to Lynn Lake, a mining town 160 kilometres south of old Brochet, to play hockey in a tournament. Usually, the girls would find their mother waiting for them at home with lunch, their father grating the lake ice — at that season a half-metre thick — free of snow, to make way for the winter road southward to Lynn Lake. When they got home that day, however, all was silent. The door was unlocked, but there was no one there to mind the home fires. They called their mother. No answer. They looked in the kitchen, the living room, the bathroom, the bedrooms. No one. Dreading the moment, they tiptoed down to the basement. And there they found her, cowering and crying in a corner, facing the wall with her hands covering her face. When she turned to her four young daughters, her eyes were black, purple, and blue, swollen to look like pincushions. So swollen were they that she was blind. The skin on her formerly beautiful, entrancing face was lacerated, torn, bloodied, as if some animal had ripped at it with angry claws.

"Divorce, separation," thundered Father Eemshaathik from his elevated perch at St. Pierre Church in old Brochet all that month, "neither is allowed by the Catholic Church."

IN THE BEGINNING, THERE WERE only two human beings in this world: Don Weegees and Bell Fontaine. At least for each other, they were the world's only human beings, that's how deeply in love they were, or thought they were, when they first met. Short but wiry, Don Weegees hailed from Southend, a larger village at the far southern end of Reindeer Lake, where it crosses over into Saskatchewan; he had recently moved the 250 kilometres north to Brochet to work in construction. Now installed in the Cree-Dene village, he lived in a house near Ma Gloire Moorah and his wife, Misty Mary, a good kilometre from the Companeek store. Bell Fontaine lived fifteen minutes behind that store, which meant she was also mere steps from the Companeek quay, where docked all bush planes; in those days, old Brochet had no airport and so was beholden to Reindeer Lake for all air travel. By chance one day, Bell Fontaine met the swaggering man with the lantern jaw named Don Weegees at the base of the quay, there to help unload cargo for the Companeek store. She was there to meet her mother, who was arriving from the hospital in Winnipeg, where she had survived a year-long bout of tuberculosis. She was sixteen; he twenty-six. They locked glances. At which point, Don Weegees started walking up the hill with Bell Fontaine and her mother to where they lived.

By the middle of that summer, Bell Fontaine had fallen in love, or thought she had, with Don Weegees. One August evening, when the moon was at its fullest and a breeze from the south made the verdure sway seductively, they paused for a spell of fifteen minutes.

Bell Fontaine got pregnant, which spelled the beginning of the end for Bell Fontaine, she of the mane of flowing black hair and twinkling eyes. At age sixteen, she got married to Don Weegees. And over the course of the next two decades, they had children. And children and children and yet more children.

Eyewitness accounts from a neighbour exist of Don Weegees running down the hill on which stood their humble little dwelling with, clutched to his chest, Bell Fontaine-now-Weegees's most precious belonging: her Singer manual sewing machine, an appliance practically impossible to come by in this extremely isolated settlement of eight hundred people. She depended on it for her life. She made her children's clothes with it, her husband's, hers. His loot in hand, Don Weegees ran down to the lake-shore with his wife in screaming pursuit, pleading with him not to destroy it. When he reached the lake, he threw it in the water, where it sank like lead. Their canoe sitting unused and empty mere metres away, Bell Fontaine-now-Weegees pushed it off the beach, jumped in, grabbed a paddle, and, with strokes most desperate, made her way to the spot where she had last seen her treasure. Her husband waded in after her, scrambled into the vessel, wrested the paddle from her hands and threw it to the side, grabbed her by the waist, and tossed her overboard. At this point in the canoe's trajectory, the water was beyond her depth. And northerners don't swim. They can't. The climate won't allow it; the summers are too brief, the water too cold, so no one ever learns. Treading water, swallowing liquid in gasps and gulps, and screaming all along like a strangled dog, Bell Fontaine-now-Weegees grabbed one gunwale of the floundering canoe with both hands and clung to it for her life, begging her husband, "Please don't do this to me. Please don't do this to me."

Did he listen? Did he show her pity? No. With every ounce of strength he could muster, he hit her fingers with the paddle, forcing her to release her hold. And she sank. And as she wriggled about like a trout caught on a fisherman's hook, he pushed her deeper into the water with the paddle, trying repeatedly with all his might to drown her. All while their six-year-old girl and four-year-old boy were standing on the beach, watching this and howling like puppies, the two-year-old girl and month-old boy too small to leave the house.

Bell Fontaine-now-Weegees somehow managed to save herself that day, or someone saved her; the details are lost in the general convulsion. But throughout that blood-freezing winter, the neighbour who witnessed this obscene perversion of the sacrament of marriage would lie on her belly on the ice and, wrapped in parka, mitts, and toque, inch her way to where she knew the sewing machine lay at lake's bottom just metres below. Aged thirteen, she was a half-Swedish, half-Cree orphan who had been adopted from an itinerant, recently widowed Swedish hermit trapper by the kind old woman who lived next door to Bell and Don Weegees. The girl cleared the snow with a mitted hand so that, as through a window, she could peer through the thick ice at the gleaming black-and-silver symbol of a marriage from which there was no exit, ever, not for Bell Weegees, not for any woman, not in the system known as monotheism.

"IN THE BEGINNING," BOOMS LIKE THUNDER the monotheistic King of the Sky from his elevated perch in swirling clouds, "there were only two human beings in this world, a man and a woman..."

The Native Trickster, however, is neither. Or both, at one and the same time, for, first and foremost, s/he is a shape-shifter. S/he can change into and be anyone or anything s/he wants at any given point in time. She can be a man, he can be a woman — the absence of gender in Cree facilitates the process — s/he can be an animal, most notably, a mangy coyote. Or a rabbit. Or a spider. She

can be a rock. He can be a piece of wood, a stick.
Like Mercury — both the chemical element and the
Roman god after whom the liquid is named — s/he
is difficult to put your finger on, as slippery a character as you are ever likely to meet.

In the story that opened this chapter, s/he is
both male and female. It comes to us from the
Blackfoot Nation of Southern Alberta, a people
much admired for their robust sense of humour.
And she appears here in her manifestation as a
coyote, or, rather, a coyote in double exposure, as
Old Man Coyote and Coyote Woman. Imagine the
Greek Hermaphrodite, double-gendered progeny
of the love goddess Aphrodite and the Trickster
god Hermes, gambolling about in the foothills
of Southern Alberta at a time long before human
beings existed.

In Cree — and, I would imagine, in Blackfoot,
an Algonquian language I don't yet speak (never
say never) — this story is knee-slappingly funny.
Listening to it, we laugh. And laugh and laugh
and laugh. We laugh until we cry. And our bodies move accordingly. But then we get hit with the
English language, and the human body instantly
ceases to jiggle. The shoulders droop, the spinal col-
umn stiffens, the mouth freezes. And that dreadful

angel — the man with wings and a sword of flame — raises his blade, and suddenly the story is no longer funny. It is like watching a punctured balloon go flaccid. Why? Because its subject is sex. Because its subject is human pleasure.

English is a brilliant language, just not when it comes to the description of pleasure. That's not its talent. Yet one of the great privileges of my life has been the opportunity to learn it. For me, it was eighteen years of pure hard labour on the one hand, but of love on the other — pure, unconditional, and full-fledged love. I *love* the Moony-ass; I've been sleeping with one — the same one — for almost four decades, so I must love them. I've learned their English language — and more! Today, I speak four Moony-ass languages and am very proud of it. But now that I've mastered English to the point where I can use it to write plays, books, and the lyrics to songs, the music for which I also write, I love it to shreds. Like all languages, English is inventive and colourful and expressive and powerful and, in the end, fascinating. And what I find most fascinating about it is the way it engages the brain in a manner that none of the other languages that I know does. Science, mathematics, finance, pursuits of the head — gymnastics of the brain, I call them — those are its fortes; that's where it thrives, where it lives. For me, after having pored through every single word and syllable of its verbal fecundity, and comparing it to the many other languages I have tried on my world travels, I find English to be the world's quintessential language of the intellect. It's brilliant. When I need money, I speak English faster than the speed of sound. And generally get it. When I try to make money in Cree, by comparison, I go hungry. Cree is terrible when it comes to making money. But laughter? Hysteria unzipped, unbound, uncorked? That's Cree's genius.

However, like all languages, English has its limits. Its Achilles heel? Its one weakness? It stops at the neck. Anything below is terra incognita or, at least, terra pericolosa ("dangerous" in Italian). The heart, the stomach, the lungs, the liver, the kidneys, the large intestine, the small intestine, the womb, the prostate, the penis, the vagina, the anus — especially the last three — one doesn't talk about them in polite company. One doesn't talk about them at all. In a word, there is nothing more terrifying to the English language than sex. If I have seen it once, I have seen it twice, I have seen it a hundred times. As a writer in the throes of a public reading in English, I'll be standing on a stage in front of fifty, a hundred, or five hundred people, and always the Trickster, always the agent provocateur, I will say something as seemingly harmless, as sweetly innocent, as "Tit's true, why would I lie to you?" And I will see a flash of pure and utter terror shoot across the surfaces of a thousand eyes at the sound of *that word*, the three-letter word in the phrase just cited that begins with a "t." It's as if the room has just been struck by God the Almighty Father's golden thunderbolt. For here he comes again, the angel with the sword of flame, swatting the oochisk of five hundred people. Oochisk? A Cree word considered off-limits in English, the inoffensive "posterior" is the closest I can get. Nichisk, kichisk, oochisk. My posterior, your posterior, his/her posterior. In one language, harmless enough — in fact, quite chaste — but nowhere near funny. In the other language? Hysterical: kichisk. The syllables alone are like a tickle in the — Well, let's not go there. It's too much fun.

Inside the polytheistic and pantheistic superstructures, the words mean pleasure. Ask Aphrodite; ask Weesaa-geechaak. Inside the monotheistic superstructure, by contrast, the speaker of the words "Tit's true" has just set one foot inside the garden, the garden of pleasure, the garden of joy, the garden of beauty that is the human body, below the neck, unclothed and unhidden. The garden of beauty from which we were evicted some four thousand years ago and at whose gate stands the angel with the flaming sword, a fearsome figure there to swat you on your bum if you dared put one foot back into that garden of pleasure with the words "tit's true." What word could be more filthy, more disgusting, more filled with evil, more expressive of self-hatred, of revulsion at the idea of the garden, of pleasure that is the human body in all its glory? Swat, and you're out of there, unsmiling, guilty, red-faced, smarting, just for uttering the dreaded three-letter word that begins with — horrors — a "t." To get beyond that fear, that hate, that revulsion, you would have to go to other languages, which is why it has been so important for me to become multilingual — to understand, implicitly and explicitly, just how functions change from one language to another, how language changes the very movements of your body, the way it makes the tension in your shoulders go from rigid to relaxed. Which is what sex is for: to relax you. Try it someday; trust me, you'll never give it up.

The problem with monotheism is that it not only misunderstands the human body; it also refuses to recognize its existence. It flatly denies biology. It sweeps it under the rug, with disastrous consequences, violence against women being the least of them, child sexual abuse being another. Why so much sexual dysfunction? Why the demonization of a liquid as powerful as semen, as exquisite, as sacred as to give life and form to the almost eight billion human beings that populate this planet today? And give so much pleasure in its distribution? It all has to do with a certain garden. If you're not allowed to go into the garden of beauty that is your body and all the joyful pleasure it holds, if you're not allowed to touch the "tree," except with guilt, guilt most twisted, guilt most monstrous, then you get sick. Which is what happens when a certain patriarchal institution, a certain monotheistic religion, dictates no sex for its priests.

In order to continue the tripartite comparison of mythologies and the languages that spring from them, to move from discussing monotheism to polytheism, I will have to resort to a second European language. I don't speak Greek, at least not yet, certainly not ancient Greek, so I will have to break the pattern here, or at least bend it and veer off somewhat. Courageously, perhaps even foolishly, I will replace the second language in our

lineup of three with one that could be said to be
the progeny of one of its languages: French. At this
point in our study, French, which is a monotheistic
language, will replace Greek, which is a polytheistic language. In this way does French, if only
for this part of my thesis, straddle two mythologies, two superstructures. A European language
I speak well enough to negotiate its pleasures, its
Gallic munificence, and avoid its pitfalls, French at
least springs from Latin. In this way, even if only
a small way, can it lay claim to certain fundamen-
tal aspects of Latin's polytheistic past. Meaning to
say that if English is the quintessential language
of the intellect, then French, more so than other
Romance languages, such as Spanish and Italian,
for example, is the quintessential language of the
heart. And of the stomach. No one — *no one* — rev-
els in the libidinous pleasures of wine, cheese, and
pâté de foie gras like the French do. If English lives
so much inside the head that it can't go past the
neck to savour the pleasures that lie on the other
side of that gate, then French lives — glories — in
that region of the body between the neck and the
waist. Hearkening back again to its polytheistic
past, it clings, if with one foot only, to the edges
of the garden of pleasure, the garden of joy, the

garden of beauty where loll with impunity the goddess Aphrodite, the gods Dionysus, Hermes, Pan,
Priapus, and all the other divinities of pleasure, of
rabid sensuality.

To give the theory an iconoclastic twist, the
Romance languages, because of their history,
political and otherwise, are Catholic languages
and thus are allowed to sin six days of the week,
on Saturday nights in particular, when Dionysus
rules and *pan*demonium lays siege to entire communities, in bars especially, so that his penitents
are then liberated to worship God the Father — or
Zeus, King of the Sky — on Sunday mornings, with
their carnal excesses forgiven, washed away like
glass that's been Windexed. Protestant languages —
English, German, and Dutch being just three of
several — don't have that privilege. Shackled by
their history — when Protestantism broke away
from the Catholic Church in the Reformation and
the rules changed drastically — they are refused
entry into that garden by the angel with the sword
of flame seven days a week, with no respite. They
have no confession, when sins are forgiven, and no
communion, when they are washed away so that
sinning — read: pleasure — can resume its wayward
journey, if gradually, from Monday to Tuesday,

until coming back to Saturday night. Which is why English stops at the neck and goes no further, whereas French can sneak in — to engage in acts of pleasure, if laced with guilt, such as eating and drinking and making love. "Oui. Tout à fait, mes chers amis. Les samedis soirs, on fait l'amour. Toujours. Avec passion."

Finally, if English is the quintessential language of the head, and French is the quintessential language of the heart (and of the stomach), then Cree is the quintessential language of the body, of that part of the body that is the most ridiculous-looking, the most clown-like, yet the most pleasurable.

Here's another story — a true story — about a different but related body part, that horrifies in one language but thrills in another. A dear friend of mine had just died, the esteemed director of three plays with whom I finally broke into the ranks of professional playwrights in Toronto, Ontario, considered the theatre capital of Canada, so I owed this man a lot. A Moony-ass man, but so madly in love did he fall with "the rez" — slang for "the reserve," as in "Indian reserve" — that I was writing about in my plays that he pulled up roots in Toronto, from where he hailed, and moved "to the island," that is, Manitoulin Island, where the aforementioned plays are set. In effect, he moved into my plays, living with "the Rez Sisters" in all their madness for a decade before he left this mortal coil. I cried and cried, as did everyone who came to his funeral, for he was beloved. He was just forty-one when he left us.

There was a service at the church down the hill, followed by a burial at the cemetery up the hill and into the forest behind the village, followed by the traditional communal meal Native people gener-ally have at the home of the deceased. The meal was served buffet-style, so everyone had to serve themselves at a big oval table that groaned with food. And everyone was dressed to the nines on this fresh, bright morning in June. The centrepiece of the banquet was a great big beaver that someone had stuffed with nuts (wink, wink) and roasted. So here were some forty people, mostly women aged twenty to ninety, making their way around the buf-fet table and piling up their plates with salads and casseroles and cheeses. Except the circle of women was moving so slowly that there was plenty of time for talk. (Get ready. In English, you'll cringe; in Cree, you'll laugh.)

"So, is it true," sweetly inquired a swarthy maiden who, apparently, had never had the pleasure of eating the animal called amik in Ojibway, amisk in Cree, "what they say about beaver?"

"What?" asked an older woman on the other side of the table, almost offended, almost defensive. "What do they say about beaver?" The subtext being, as it always is in any and all Indigenous languages, "What are they saying about *my* beaver?"

"That young beaver is tender and juicy," replied the young woman with a voice as melodious as a young peepeek-sees (robin). "And old beaver is tough and rubbery." Here, for some reason, she gave the older woman an accusatory look.

As it turned out, the women standing in line on one side of the table were of the older generation, aged fifty to ninety, give or take a decade, while the women on the other side were sixteen to thirty — in effect, the younger generation. A lively debate ensued about the merits of young beaver compared to those of old beaver. The volume rose, knives were raised, forks flashed, and fists gesticulated, for the argument was fierce. In fact, there was so much movement at that table that the beaver at its middle shook and rattled and rocked and rolled until, finally, a ninety-year-old woman silenced the lot by declaring: "Old beaver may be tough and rubbery, but it's much better than young beaver.

Trust me, Mildred. I know whereof I speak." And the older women won.

These were not leering old men; they were ordinary Indigenous women, who have a great sense of humour, as does the entire rez, as does the culture in its near entirety (trust me, not all Native people are funny). This is an example of a perfectly ordinary conversation at an Indigenous banquet table in modern times. It may be ordinary, yes, and it may be modern, but it is Indigenous. Meaning that each and every one of its clown-like syllables has the rhythm of the Trickster motoring it. The laughter was universal and long and ringing — and this was a funeral, for God's sake! A toast was made to the expired animal, even if all that was left of its former succulence was its skeleton, its Ping-Pong-paddle tail, and its teeth, for beaver is eaten on reserves with vim and with vigour. And as often as possible. Off-reserve? No. You would never be caught dead eating beaver — young, old, or middle-aged. In Toronto? Unthinkable.

THE NEXT FEATURE THAT DISTINGUISHES these three mythologies one from the other is the manner in which they view gender. Languages that come from monotheistic systems divide the universe into two genders. In English there is he and she and her and him and his and hers. But barring exceptions, and strictly speaking, nouns themselves have no gender. Nouns are neither she nor he; they have, instead, been relegated to a kind of collective non-gender status called neuter; a stone, for example, is an "it," a tree is an "it," a road is an "it." Exceptions are vehicular terms such as boats, planes, and cars ("Ain't she a beaut?") and whales ("Thar she blows") and men and women and boys and girls and cats and dogs. And there are others, just not that many.

Every French noun, by contrast — and this is yanking that language from its former purpose in the world of polytheism back into the world of monotheism — has to be preceded by either a masculine article ("le") or its feminine equivalent ("la"). There is, however, and strictly speaking, no neuter; that is to say, no such word as "it" exists in the language. To add insult to injury, most positive ideas are masculine, as in love ("l'amour"), happiness ("le bonheur"), and laugh ("un rire"), and negative ideas are female, as in "la tristesse" (sadness), "la douleur" (pain), and "la mort" (death). So anti-woman is this language that the only way a man can have a feminine identity is to be a victim ("une victime"), a target ("une cible"), or a criminal ("une criminelle"). Contrariwise, anything remotely positive on the female corpus is masculine, the vagina ("un vagin") being a sterling example. In Italian, Spanish, and Portuguese, including in its Brazilian incarnation, the organ is as feminine as lipstick. "Let me have a look," said a female Brazilian friend in a bar in Rio de Janeiro one steamy evening some dozen years ago, *Cristo Redentor*, the world-famous giant statue of Jesus, floating in the night sky high above us. Shocked to discover that French vaginas are masculine, she marched to the washroom, was gone for a spell, and came back beaming. "I'm happy to announce," she ululated in her sexy, samba-inflected Portuguese, "that my vagina is feminine." We roundly toasted the star-crossed organ.

It's a minefield, this matter of gender. At one sitting in a bistro in Paris, France, or Val-d'Or, Quebec, you can eat, in order, an apple, a turnip, a carrot, a cucumber, and a shrimp, and you will have just consumed an object that, in order, is feminine ("une pomme"), masculine ("un navet"), feminine ("une carrotte"), masculine ("un concombre"), and feminine ("une crevette"). By the end of the meal, your head is spinning and your lower regions are

making unseemly noises. And your mind is won-
dering: Is meat masculine? It is not. Even if it comes
from a steer, it is still feminine; even excrement
that comes from a man is feminine! What about a
cake? What about a pie? In French a cake is masculine, but a pie is feminine. Yet the eight items
of food just listed are all just that — items of food!

We'll go one step deeper . . . The languages of
monotheistic mythology position all nouns according to a hierarchy of power represented by a straight
line standing vertical. At the very summit of that
hierarchy sits God as Male with an uppercase "M."
One step down comes man with a lowercase "m."
Then comes woman with a lowercase "f." And last
comes nature, which has neither "M" nor "m" nor
"f" but is neuter; that is to say, it has no gender.
The design of this structure is phallic — that is, a
straight line standing up. And in this phallic construction, man has total and complete power over
woman. To give it a biblical spin, she is nothing
but the rib bone of her husband, a stick of furniture in his house. And both genders have complete
power over nature. There is, moreover, room on
that straight line for two genders only: male and
female, and never the twain shall meet. Anyone
who dares cross that gender divide pays dearly for

it. Millions have died grotesque and horrifying deaths for engaging in such an act. In many regions of the world, they are still hunted down like animals. Finally, where on that phallic straight line is the female with an uppercase "F"? The answer is: nowhere. The concept simply does not exist, that's how absent the female principle is from monotheism. That's how patriarchal the system.

If the monotheistic system of thought delineates a straight line standing vertical, then the polytheistic system delineates a semicircle, a curve of sorts. Ancient Greek has genders — masculine, feminine, and neuter — but there is no hierarchy. All gods and goddesses in the pantheon of twelve sit at the same debating half-table, at a level that is equal. Chairing duties would be shared by Father Sky Zeus and his wife, Mother Earth Hera, and the other ten deities — five female, five male — would have an equal voice at the meeting because not one among them was sitting higher than any other. Fittingly, it was a more democratic system, one where woman actually had a voice. And homosexuality was practised openly — if you don't believe me, read Plato's *Symposium*.

If there is room for two genders only on the straight line of monotheism, and three genders on

the semicircle of polytheism, then the circle of pantheism has space for any number of genders. On
the circle of Mother Earth in Indigenous mythology, heterosexual woman was, strictly speaking,
biologically equipped for the act of giving birth;
my mother had twelve children, of whom I am the
eleventh. Therefore, she sits on the first side of the
circle. Heterosexual man, in the sense most traditional, was biologically equipped for the hunt and
feeding his family, so he sits on the third side of the
circle. My father was a legendary hunter; he gave
chase to entire herds of caribou like no other man.

And then there are those people who are
equipped for neither role. Indigenous peoples
have a beautiful, all-inclusive name for them in
English: Two-Spirits. Whether they came into this
world male or female biologically, they are people
who have the souls of both genders at one and
the same time. In English and related monotheistic languages, such people have ugly, derogatory,
exclusionary names filled with hatred; they are
considered people who should best be exterminated as quickly as possible. Instead, Two-Spirits sit
with honour on the second and fourth sides of the
all-encompassing circle of pantheism and so must
serve a useful purpose. If they can't, for example,

hunt or give birth, in the traditional ways, then their role is to care for the spiritual life of the community. They are the shamans and priests of the community. And the artists, the visionaries.

Another role Two-Spirits fill? Because the heterosexual male and heterosexual female are generally busy raising their children and making a living to feed those children — in olden times, they would sometimes have ten, twelve, fourteen; my dad's youngest brother, my uncle Adam Highway, had twenty-two children! — they don't always have time to care for their young. So we make great babysitters, great aunts and uncles. What's more, we take care of the aged, who are all too frequently abandoned by their children in homes for seniors, stashed away in a drawer to wait for death. In the south of France, where my partner and I lived for fourteen unforgettable winters, the town we chose, right where the Pyrenees Mountains meet the Mediterranean Sea, was, in essence, a retirement village. It was filled with very old people, frequently with only children who seldom, or never, came to visit them. To take their place, my partner of almost forty years played bridge with them almost every day, both in that village and in others up and down the coast. And if they didn't know how, he, an international-level bridge player, taught them. Mostly abandoned by their families, these seniors often had only their animals for company. In this landscape difficult to negotiate on foot, with hills everywhere, their extreme age prevented them from stooping to the sidewalk to pick up after their animals. So do you know who followed them with a plastic bag and cleaned up after them? My partner. *That's* the job of a real Two-Spirit: a holy person born into this world with the souls of both male and female and who is thus frequently the wielder of magic powers available in no other way. Every family should be so blessed as to have at least one such person.

Last, Two-Spirits act as a buffer between the two eternally warring opposing genders of heterosexual male and heterosexual female that make for a world that is not only boring but lethally dangerous for gays and women. If women stand to get raped just by walking down a street, then Two-Spirit people stand to get killed. And do. My own life has been threatened three times already, once by a beating by four gay-bashers in a poorly lit, isolated parking lot behind the Manitoba legislature, once by a van that tried to run me over, and once by attempted arson, while I was scrawling out, longhand, late at night, an early draft of a play that would come to be known as *The Rez Sisters*.

The monotheistic world of two genders is black and white. But the whole world cries out for colour. And we Two-Spirits bring that colour, which is why we fly the rainbow flag! I like to put it this way: without this gender, what would Cher have to wear? There is nothing — nothing! — more exciting than a Two-Spirit party. And there is nothing more exciting, more passionate, more fulfilling than a friendship between a heterosexual woman and a Two-Spirit man. Heterosexual men and women too rarely speak the same emotional language. Gay men and straight women do, and they do so with an emotional fire and electricity that makes them the best friends in the world. Countless times have I seen — on a city bus, on the subway, on the street — a lonely old woman, who would otherwise be dying in a loveless and only too frequently abusive marriage, laughing uproariously with one of those queenly, totally effeminate men who would have been killed a long time ago by gay-bashers. Two total rejects from society, according, at least, to the system called monotheism, having the time of their lives is liberation, all-out happiness. The love between them is palpable.

Within the full circle of Indigenous mythology, the universe is not divided into that which is male, female, and neuter, but according to that which is animate and that which is inanimate, that which has a soul and that which has not. According to this system, woman has a soul, as does a man as does a bear as does a cow as does a tree as does a rock, the definite article being "ana" (as with all two-syllable words in Cree, the stress is always on the second syllable, as in "aha"). Applied to the "beings" just named, the article, and the noun it applies to, go: ana isk'wao (woman), ana napao (man), ana maskwa (bear), ana moostoos (cow), ana seeti (tree), ana asini (rock) — what would be the "le" and "la" in French. They are all animate; they all have souls. And there is most explicitly no hierarchy, no straight line, no phallic design. There is, instead, a full circle, a yonic design. Yonic? A word from Sanskrit, the sacred language of Hindu philosophy and of the historical texts of Buddhism, it means "vagina like."

All these animate beings sit on one side of the circular debating table. And because they all, as with the Greek gods and goddesses, sit at the same level, they have an equal voice in the discussion. At this table, woman is most assuredly not the rib bone of her husband; in fact, if anyone is a rib bone of anyone, it is the husband, of his wife. The only way to remove the soul from these beings is to kill them, at which point the defining article becomes "anima": both woman and man become anima meeyow (the corpse), the bear becomes anima anaas-kaan (the carpet), the cow becomes anima weeyaas (the meat), the tree becomes anima teeta-poowin (a chair; that is, a chair is a tree with the soul removed), and the rock becomes anima meeska-now (a sidewalk).

When you apply this equation to the various parts of the human body individually, you find, very quickly, that each and every one of them has no soul. They are all inanimate, mere lifeless objects. Anima misti-g'wan (head), anima michee-chi (hand), anima misit (foot), anima watay (stomach), even anima miti (heart) — all have no soul, no spirit. Even the penis by itself has no soul. The testicles do, however, but that's because the Cree word for them is assin-iyak, which means rocks. The only two parts of the human body that, by themselves, have a soul are the womb and the vagina. And there lies the seed of the idea that divinity is female. That idea lies at the very core of our languages and thus our mythological superstructure. That's where lies the seed of the idea of matriarchy. That's where exists, and exists most vividly, the uppercase "F" of female, right smack dab at the heart of that circle, that womb.

Oh, pardon me. There is one more human organ that by itself has a soul. It is uncomfortable to explain in English, but I'll give you four hints: 1. Both male and female bodies have it. 2. It is the most ridiculous-looking part of the human body yet the most amusing, the most pleasurable. 3. It makes great music. 4. In the West today, we are bearing witness to a rising epidemic of a fatal ailment, a crucial factor for which might be the act of, well, flatulence, or the suppression thereof.

Still don't get it? It's the place where rules supreme Weesaa-geechaak and his army of Tricksters. Kipoo-chim, we call it. Try saying the word in the mirror. Or in front of your lover. Or to yourself as you fall asleep at night. Kipoo-chim has the same rhythm as chikaboom. The syllables alone will make you chortle yourself to sleep. You will sleep twice as well. And feel all the better the next day — let 'er rip!

FIVE

On Death

AT THE FRONT OF THE CLASSROOM stands Father
Cheepootaat, our skinny-as-a-rail, red-haired,
pot-bellied catechism teacher, in his flowing black
cassock, waving his wooden pointer this way and
that to indicate God up in heaven, with his cotton-
candy beard, his bulbous belly, and his golden
sceptre, a jagged thunderbolt that flashes and
glints in a peerless sun. That's the image of God
the Father that was drilled into me at the Guy Hill
Indian Residential School, where I spent nine years
as a hard-working student. The priest's name was
actually Thiboudeau, but Cheepootaat was the closest we could get with our children's tongues that
spoke Cree to begin with, not French, not English.
Cheep'wow means "pointy" in Cree, for the priest

had a nose that looked like a stinger, on a hornet, for example. The second part of his name is derived from the verb eemataat, the meaning of which you don't want to know. Let's put it this way and leave it at that: the English language won't let you go there...

And this heaven teems with "angels," Father Cheepootaat informs us with his raspy throat and darting ootee-thani (tongue), "servants of God, messengers, that kind of thing."

These winged men are as numerous as the clouds and cowboy handsome, with long blond hair and streamlined bodies, as though they go to God's gymnasium to stretch their muscles on a basis semi-regular.

"And cooks?" Bobby Moose, a boy in my class, has the gumption to inquire. "Cleaners?"

"Yes," says the priest, with a face as expressionless as mud, then he soldiers on with the lesson.

In monotheism, when a person comes to the end of the straight line of the life as he has lived it for a length of time, whether that time be five or sixty or a hundred years, his spirit leaves his body and floats like vapour, or so it is said, to heights unheard of, at least by us mortals still alive and breathing upon this planet. Once thus liberated, however, that spirit doesn't travel by itself. Whether the deceased has died in a car crash or of cancer in a bed in a hospital room or by drowning in a river, an angel — a man with wings that rival in beauty the wings of swans — swoops down from the blue and wondrous sky yonder, on the highway where his car was hit or at his bedside in downtown Toronto, as was the case with my late younger brother, or in the river where floats his body, to escort him to … Well, that's the problem, for this spirit-as-vapour finds itself confronting three options and learns, moreover, that the choice is not his to make. Someone else decides: a deity, a god called Father. He will decide which route the recently deceased takes. Which is the first step in the worrisome and frequently terrifying part of a journey that will take him to the end of time. Will he go to heaven? Or will he go to hell? Or will he go to a place in the middle called purgatory?

In my child's dream world, the colour white is omnipresent in this place called heaven: the clouds — clouds far as the naked human eye can penetrate, as though seen from a plane — and the wings on angels who wear sheet-white robes, all ankle-length with full-length sleeves, their skins, their complexions, all white as Five Roses Flour. Not a single one of them is Black, it dawns on me, at least not on this chart that Father Cheepootaat shows us in class. And no one is yellow. And no one is brown or red, not like us Cree. The only objects that are not white in this heaven are the throne on which sits "his majesty," his afore-mentioned thunderbolt, and the harps, as Father Cheepootaat gamely explains the ornate instru-ments with strings the thinness of clotheslines, all of which are golden with hints of silver. Every angel holds one of these kitoo-chiga-nak (musical instruments), and they pluck those strings, these men with wings, and make sweet music in four-four time, says the red-haired priest with a small pot-belly that looks like a lapwachin hidden under his cassock. A lapwachin is a pudding that is boiled in a bag but looks like fruitcake because of its rai-sins. As with so many Cree words with French and English origins, it is a corruption of the French for pudding, pronounced "la poo-jing." In this heaven, music in three-four time is forbidden: too sugges-tive of a country waltz, says Father Cheepootaat, where people touch each other in unlikely places (whatever that means) — and they sing hymns of glory, of love, of praise to Gitche Manitou, as he calls our dear K'si-mantoo. And smoking is for-bidden, as is drinking, as is sex, I learn years later.

And there is not a twitch of evil or sadness or depression or thoughts suicidal — or women, for that matter — in that lofty environment, says the priest. In fact, only priests and bishops and popes, who are all Catholic, are allowed in. For there is room only for happiness inviolate, happiness eternal, happiness impossible to crush or to annihilate. "Keechi-geesi-gook" Father Cheepootaat says it is called in our language: "The Great Sky." Whatever name this place called heaven has in whatever language, it is the first choice for those who have earned their right to enter it, where they will kneel at the right hand of this God the Father for eternity.

"That's a lot of kneeling," I've been thinking for years, unsure I will like this place. My poor little brother, who died at thirty-five some thirty years ago, with his purity of spirit and his awesome humility, in spite of his jaw-dropping beauty, surely he has earned his entry into "the Kingdom of God," even if he has to kneel for ten million years. As have, surely, my mother and father. No one deserved entry into heaven more than they, except that my father was an accordionist not a harpist, as I inform the priest in class that day.

"Will God let my father in?" I ask this Father

Cheepootaat-which-rhymes-with-eemataat (which is what I sometimes call him to myself).

"No," snaps Father Cheepootaat. "Sorry. Accordions are not allowed in heaven."

Distraught that my father might have to change instruments or go to hell, I vow to help him keep his accordion.

The second option offered to the recently deceased by this patriarchal god is a place called purgatory. The concept of purgatory has encountered controversy for several centuries. It has been cancelled and it has been reinstated, then cancelled again, then reinstated. It's all been a terrible wrangle among theologians both Catholic and otherwise. When Protestantism first came to the fore in the sixteenth century, the new religion would have nothing to do with it, in part because of Protestantism's wholesale rejection of all things Roman Catholic, and the theory bit the dust. But then certain factions brought it back; yet even certain factions within Catholicism reject it to this day.

Whatever the dynamics of this theological earthquake, the original premise was that if you had been a man of seamless integrity, if you had led a life unmarked by vice — which is unlikely, for no one is perfect, not even the Pope — then your winged escort would take you in his arms and bear you straight to the airy heights of heaven, where, ensconced on a throne constructed out of gold, sits the monotheistic God the Father. Those who hadn't led a perfect life, which is most, wouldn't be allowed entry into heaven, where the few perfect people went. But the sins of those many imperfect people hadn't been serious enough to send them to hell, which is the opposite of heaven. So they would be admitted into this sort of way station where they could cleanse — that is, purge — themselves of whatever sins they had committed while still living. And the length of time it took to do that depended on the number of sins and their gravity. If you'd stolen ten dollars from the collection plate at church, it could be a month. If you'd killed a neighbour's dog, it could be a year. If you'd been a habitual liar, it could be a hundred. If you'd ruined someone's career by slandering their name, it could be a thousand. Committing adultery, carrying out extortion, evading your taxes — they all counted against you. Still, you could undergo a process of penitence and be forgiven, eventually. That penitence? A string of Hail Marys as long as day, recited on your knees until they creaked.

At which point, you could continue on to heaven.
There is, however, no physical description existent
anywhere of this fascinating place called purgatory. As Father Cheepootaat once said from his
pulpit on Sunday, "It is not a place but a soul state."
For a place with a physical description, you must
go to heaven. Or hell.

But first, limbo, which is not a dance but another
soul state.

"Oh, it's somewhere out there," said Father
Cheepootaat with a yawn that said, *What do I care?*

It turned out limbo was only for unbaptized
babies, a place where they would not be in communion with God but would nonetheless enjoy
happiness eternal. But then Pope Benedict XVI cancelled it in 2007. I have always imagined limbo as a
giant hockey puck, black as slate, twirling through
space with a million dead babies trapped inside it.
And now those babies are doomed to twirl through
space forever.

And now to hell. If you, for example, killed your
husband, or shot twenty people in a schoolyard
massacre, or were responsible for the deaths of ten
million people in a war, then you, at the moment of
death, were bound for hell. Whether your remains
were lying in a bed at a hospital, burnt to a cinder

in a terrible inferno, or crushed under a fridge, your spirit would be extracted from your heart by a devil — another man with wings but this one red not white — handcuffed, shackled, and then dragged down a tunnel, kicking and shrieking until the walls are ringing, to a cave called hell. And those devils are the embodiment of evil. According to the map that Father Cheepootaat showed us at boarding school, these devils are stark naked, with skin redder than a Santa costume, with snake-like tails that writhe and coil and come to a fork at the tip, and the horns and hooves of a goat — significantly, just like Pan, the Greek god of pleasure.

These demons were once angels, part of the ranks that included luminaries such as the Archangels Michael, Gabriel, and Raphael. They are disillusioned angels who made the mistake of following a leader, Lucifer by name, an angel himself, an arrogant incendiary who dared doubt God's peerless intelligence, claiming he was more deserving of the title King of Heaven than his father. For this heresy, Lucifer and his henchmen were thrown out of heaven; by the tens of thousands, they fell from the heights and plunged down to Earth and beyond, down, down, and down, until they reached its crust, where they have been living ever since in

a cavern that is a noxious, belching, raging inferno.
Flame and flame and yet more flame.

And the King of Hell, Lucifer himself — sometimes called Satan — sits on his throne at the centre
of it all, his sceptre a trident, a three-pronged fork I
have always been convinced he stole from Poseidon,
Greek god of the sea. And from his elevated position, he oversees the torture of his trillions of
victims, which, according to the vision of hell
espoused by Father Cheepootaat, includes all those
accordion players playing a joyful, jigging, chikaboom sort of music. Ah yes, the music, not just
hymns to the glory of God in four-four time but
rhythm and blues and jazz and rock and roll, blues,
Tin Pan Alley, stride, honky-tonk, salsa, samba,
rumba, mambo, limbo, bingo, dingo, jingo, polka;
they're all there, in three-four time, in six-eight
time, in seven-eight, three-eight, nine-eight time.
And the makers of that music are being pierced
with tridents day after day after day and thrown
like scraps of meat into a pile of burning, scorched
bodies writhing in agony and screaming unthinkable, unprintable epithets. And smoking, drinking,
and sex are not only allowed but encouraged, as
I will learn years later.

No other mythology has an uglier, more twisted,

more perverted vision of the afterlife. It is guaranteed to terrify us all into submission here in this life, where we must suffer as much as we can. And you wonder why death in the monotheistic system is a terrifying prospect, a bone-crushing trauma.

"Chances are," Father Cheepootaat once intoned at an altar boy who had been caught stealing sacramental wine from the priest's stash in the sacristy, a sort of backstage behind the altar, "chances are that you, Chaggy What Custard, will go straight to hell upon your death and burn there forever!" (The boy's last name was actually Custer, but that was the state of our English back then.) And Father Cheepootaat tapped his pointer with glee at yet another chart sitting on an easel at the front of the classroom, this one depicting hell, with Satan and its entire population of red-skinned people. Ten-year-old Chaggy What Custard, who wasn't very smart to begin with, trembled in his cassock, scared to death of death until the day he ... well, until the day he died.

AS FOR THE GREEKS, they believed that at the moment of death, the psyche, or spirit of the dead, left the body as a little puff of wind. The deceased was then prepared for burial according to time-honoured rituals. Ancient literary sources refer to the omission of burial rites as an insult to human dignity. Relatives of the recently departed, primarily the women, conducted the rituals that customarily had three parts: the laying out of the body, the funeral procession, and the interment of either the body or cremated remains. After being washed and anointed with oil, the body was dressed and placed on a high bed inside the house. During the laying out, friends and relatives came to mourn and pay their respects. Lamentation of the dead is featured in Greek art at least as early as the period 900 to 700 BCE, when vases were decorated with scenes portraying the deceased surrounded by mourners. The body would then be brought to the cemetery in a ritual procession that usually took place just before dawn. Very few objects were placed in the grave, but monumental earth mounds, rectangular tombs, and elaborate marble monuments and statues were often erected to mark the grave and ensure that the deceased would not be forgotten. Immortality lay in the continued remembrance of the dead by the living. The women of Classical Athens, for instance, would make regular visits to graves with offerings that included small cakes and libations.

The most lavish funerary monuments were erected in the sixth century BCE by aristocratic families of Attica in private burial grounds along the roadside on the family estate or near Athens. Elaborate sculptures with epitaphs in verse marked many of these graves. Many of the finest Attica grave monuments stood in a cemetery located on the northwest edge of Athens, just outside the gates of the ancient city wall. The cemetery had been in use for centuries.

If the monotheistic take on the afterlife depicts three possible destinations — heaven, hell, and purgatory — then its polytheistic equivalent depicts one only, known as Hades. In his epic poem *The Odyssey*, Homer describes Hades, the place deep beneath the Earth's crust where Hades, the brother of Zeus, god of the sky, and Poseidon, god of the sea, reigns with his wife, Persephone, over crowds of countless drifting, shadowy figures — the shades of all those who have died. Hades, the place, has been described as a limbo where time disappears and the dead fade into a kind of non-being. There is no punishment and therefore no suffering. And no reward. But it is not a happy place. Indeed, the ghost of the hero Achilles told Odysseus he would rather be a poor serf on Earth than lord of all the dead in the Underworld.

In polytheistic mythology, the soul of the dead, whether sinful or not, is met by a god, at the bed in the hospital, in the crumpled car after the accident, in the river after the drowning, and escorted from the surface of the Earth to the banks of a river called the Styx. There he must pay the ferry operator, an old man named Charon, a coin that the deceased's kin would have left under his tongue, so that Charon would transport him across the water to Hades. At the gate, though, he first has to bypass the guardian of the Underworld, a ferocious three-headed dog named Cerberus. Finally, he enters this shadowy place where time is non-existent and where he will stay in a state of suspended animation for eternity. That escort god is Hermes. Offspring of Father Sky Zeus and Maia, a goddess who was one of the cluster of seven stars called the Pleiades, he has many roles and wears many guises. Among his functions are messenger of the gods; protector of human health; patron saint of travellers, thieves, and merchants; god of boundaries; and mediator between the visible and the invisible, between the conscious and the unconscious, bringer of dreams. He had shamanistic attributes, a kind of angel who is usually portrayed as a fleet young man wearing winged sandals and a winged helmet and carrying a caduceus, a sort of wand or shepherd's staff with two mating snakes writhing around it, an ancient symbol for healing. Cunning, treacherous, and scheming, Hermes is the closest figure the ancient Greeks had to a Trickster god of the sort that anchors Indigenous mythology.

LAST, HERE IS THE INDIGENOUS TAKE on what happens to the living at and after the moment of death. Always curious, the Native Trickster — Greece's Hermes, Rome's Mercury — decided he wanted to travel to the land of the dead to see what it was like, so he asked his best friend Eagle to go with him. In the guise of the animal Coyote, Trickster walked and ran while Eagle flew high above him. And as they travelled, they talked: about life, about death, and about what happens when one dies. They journeyed up and down many rivers and across many lakes where Trickster had to swim, and over hills and mountains and across many valleys and through one forest after another and even, on occasion, deserts, for the land they lived on was beautiful indeed, rich in landscape, rich in plant and animal life. So far did they have to travel and for so many days and nights that Trickster would get tired, so tired that his friend, this magnificent bird with wings like sails, would have to carry him on his back.

Eventually, they came upon an island where they heard people singing. This piqued their interest, so they swerved toward it. When they got closer, they realized that the voices, which were human, were accompanied by a drum that sounded like a heart-beat. And the singers were enveloped by a mist that swirled and billowed, for, night having fallen, it was dark. In some versions of the story, the lowly frog is suspended in the air, holding the moon to provide some light, beating all along at its surface with a drumstick.

This is how Trickster and Eagle heard the dead sing and saw them dance. For it was they who were chanting, a pentatonic chant sung in unison in voices male and female and child, for there were many children among them. They were astonished to recognize, one after another after another, their ancestors who had died going back generations, and it made them cry with an aching longing, for they wanted so dearly to stay there with them, but they couldn't. Something told them that they were not allowed, that they would have to leave by day-break. Some even say that a certain energy pulled them away.

Daybreak came and night came to an end and the mist swallowed dancer after dancer after dancer, until all sign of life on that island disappeared. Weeping tears so copious that the level of the lakes and the rivers rose, or so it is said, Trickster had no choice but to leave with his dear friend Eagle and return to the land of the living.

In the pantheistic superstructure of Indigenous mythology, when a person dies, he doesn't climb the straight line up to heaven or descend the one that leads down to hell. He doesn't even go to a place-without-time called Hades. Neither heaven nor hell nor Hades exists as a physical place in our collective subconscious, our collective dream world. Quite by contrast, in the pantheistic system, heaven and hell and Hades exist right here on this Earth, smack in the middle of that circle that is our garden, the one we were given the responsibility to care for when we came into this world as newborns. When you die, your physical self, formerly animate, becomes inanimate and merely melts into the Earth and becomes one with it. And "it" is the right word, for the Cree noun for Earth — aski — is inanimate. It is not "ana aski" but "anima aski." Even the Earth by itself — that is, without its animate beings: humans, animals, plants — is soulless, just like your head without your spirit to go with it, or your lung or your stomach or your heart. At the point of death, your physical self melts into the Earth and, over a timeline of years and years, becomes one with it. It becomes the Earth. And over a continuing timeline of years and years, it gets transformed into flesh, of plants, insects, animals, human beings — that is, *other* human beings, a new generation, your children, your children's children, your children's children's children … Which is how you find yourself, again, on the animate side of that same circle with the other living beings for a certain length of time. And thus does the circle of life and death and rebirth and life and death and rebirth and life and death continue ad infinitum. If the straight line of the patriarchal God will eventually come to an end that is definite — and it's only a matter of time — then the circle of his matriarchal equivalent doesn't.

In terms mythological, when you die, your spirit sheds its body and leaves that side of the circle where sit the animate beings — that is, the ones with living spirits — and, ostensibly under the guidance of the clown called Trickster, crosses over to the other side of that circle to sit with the inanimate beings — that is, the soulless ones — and simply goes on existing on another plain entirely, a plain that can be explained biologically, scientifically. But your spirit is still here on this planet. It hasn't left; it hasn't gone anywhere. There is nothing sentimental or delusional about it; biology can prove it. The bodies of your mother or your grandfather or your daughter or your best friend who died last year have simply melted back into the soil and, some five decades later — or ten or thirty or one hundred — come back to the land of the living as a blade of grass in a farmer's field, as the leaf shuddering on the branch of the maple tree in your front yard, as that ray of sunshine that drifts through your kitchen window and winds itself around your forearm as you're washing the dishes, as the wind that passes through your lungs to give your body marvellous movement. These are all your loved ones coming to bless you and tell you they love you. Thus, death in pantheistic superstructures is not a tragedy, it is not a traumatic event, it is not an ending. It is, rather, a beautiful passage, the most breathtaking passage you will ever take in what one hopes will be a long and happy life enriched by the laughter of a certain clown.

This is true where Native life is still at its most untouched, at its most pristine. In far subarctic Manitoba, where I grew up — not on the reserve called Barren Lands, the administrative centre of which is a village of eight hundred people called Brochet — but out on the land. It was paradise. Alone with my family amid the vista of ten thousand blue-watered lakes and endless forests and eskers, and caribou that come thundering down from the high Arctic regions in high mid-winter in herds of thousands, it was paradise. Eskers are land formations made by the movement of glaciers as they retreated to the Arctic at the end of the ice age. Snaking their way northward, as if giant moles had dug very long tunnels, they are ridges of sandy terrain that can be as high as fifty metres and as long as three hundred kilometres. Forests of spruce and pine cling to their sides, until they reach the top, where long, narrow meadows of fine golden sand take over. Golf courses floating in the clouds, they are breathtaking to look at, paradise to hike on in summer. And paradise it still is, still unseen, untouched by humans, except by us, the Highway family, and sundry Dene. Every element of life was ruled by the circle of Nature. The ride was smooth; the ride was heavenly.

The part that is more than a bit sentimental, some would even claim completely delusional, about this rosy vision of Native life here in Canada is that the social reality of Native people today doesn't reflect it. You take the Native out of such an environment and you are asking for trouble. You plunk them down in an urban environment where all is governed by the straight line — sky-high towers, streets, machines such as cars, computers, and television sets — the result, too frequently, is not very healthy, not very happy. Social breakdown on a massive scale, family breakdown, youth crime, alcohol abuse, cheap drugs, extreme poverty, all-out confusion, all-out unhappiness, despair, and suicide are all trials that bedevil the lives of downtown cores in cities the world over. Hell here on Earth, they have been called.

The reasons for this state of affairs are legion — Indigenous collective racial memory of this catalogue of misery, this collective crime of the dreaded human race, that part of it, at least, that fled the horrors of European history.

American cowboys in the "Wild West" of the nineteenth century shot "Indians," as European settlers were moving west, just to see how high their bodies would fly. It was a sport.

Germ warfare: colonizers infected us with smallpox blankets, by the hundreds of thousands. Millions of people, entire families, lost their lives.

Governments stole the most beautiful parts of our land (read: the richest) and confined us to "Indian reserves," almost always land that was worthless, untillable.

The Catholic Church held debates at the time of the Italian Renaissance (renaissance is supposed to mean a new modern way of thinking about the world and humanity's place in it that replaces a backward old one)—the fourteenth to seventeenth centuries—about whether Native North Americans had souls.

The brutal treatment of Black people in the American South affected us—we fled by the thousands before they hanged us, too.

The Catholic Church converted us by telling us that worshipping nature—worshipping a tree—was tantamount to devil worship. Spiritual extortion is what some call it. The Church terrified us into submission by feeding our children horrifying images of a hell that did not exist. Sometime in the first half of the twentieth century, the local missionary priest in Brochet at the time, Father Eemshaa-thik, once asked a Dene girl of not much more than ten years of age, "What is the most miraculous thing one can see in this life?"

"The caribou," answered the girl, in her Native Dene.

Arrogantly, the old priest chortled, "No, my dear, no. It is the angels."

In the guise of God's servant, he was telling a lie. She was telling the truth. This kind of subversion, this kind of brainwashing, nipped at the root of our spiritualism, our philosophical ideas, which is why they had to go underground and hide, simmering there for decades.

What could have been if this world view, this ideology, this collective subconscious, this pantheistic Indigenous mythology, had been listened to, if it had been respected? And what if it's too late now?

When I was growing up in the 1950s, Northern Manitoba knew few forest fires. Two or three every summer perhaps, and they were small and caused no great danger to the residents of those forests, including the animals. Even then, so vast is the land that we weren't even aware of those that happened. And there were very few people. A First Nation here with a population of eight hundred people, a First Nation there with a population of a thousand people, the two so far apart, at a time when travel was limited to canoe and dogsled and the occasional bush plane. They might as well have been the only settlements on Earth, which means emergency evacuations of entire communities by bush plane with pontoons — and, now that we have airports, planes with wheels — was unknown; there weren't any.

But now there are dozens upon dozens. Every summer the North is besieged with one forest fire after another; it is no longer safe for people or animals to live there. And not just in Manitoba but in Saskatchewan, Ontario, Alberta, and British Columbia. Emergency airlifts of entire villages, entire towns, are par for the course. From April 1, 2021, to March 28, 2022, for example, 1,642 wildfires burned 869,279 hectares of land in British Columbia alone. Towns like Lytton were burnt to the ground: people lost their houses; people lost everything. Kelowna, BC; Lesser Slave Lake, Alberta; Leaf Rapids, Manitoba; all of California, all of Australia — the list grows longer as these forest fires transpire with increasing regularity and size with every passing summer. And they're getting ever closer to the major urban centres. And then there are the floods. And the summers that get hotter and hotter. And hotter and hotter...What can we do before it's too late, before climate change devours the planet with fire or with water in one summer?

My partner and I live in the Aylmer sector of

Gatineau, a city nearing a population of three hundred thousand in the province of Quebec, right across the Ottawa River from our nation's capital. Until 2002, Aylmer was its own municipality separated from the main part of Gatineau, which used to be called Hull, by some ten kilometres of maple forest, the Ottawa River, and to-die-for bicycle paths. The pocket of Aylmer where our house is located is called Wychwood. A riverside quarter cut off from the rest of Aylmer by a major thoroughfare, it retains the feel of a country village whose history dates back to the nineteenth century; it feels very "period," very "colonial Quebec." In fact, it once was cottage country for the well-heeled of Ottawa. You can tell that every second house was a former cottage that's been spruced up to meet with modern standards of living. The telltale sign? They have no basements.

A five-minute walk from our house and you're on the river, which widens at this point out to a great big lake. Almost every street that runs perpendicular to that river — or rather, that lake — thus ends its journey at Le Lac Deschênes (the Lake of the Oaks). The result? Tiny little beaches, though not with sand but with stones, or rocks the size of baseballs, line that shoreline. And since the neighbourhood is a-clutter with civic-minded people of a certain age — Wychwood, in effect, is a retirement community — mindful residents have left Adirondack chairs and other kinds of patio furniture at intervals irregular all along the shore. It's bliss when you sit there with a chilled beer on a warm summer evening, listening to the river flowing by, sometimes with your feet right in the water.

Our grandchildren, who live with their parents some twelve blocks east of us, love to play here whenever they're over, which is often. They love picking up stones and throwing them into the river so see how many times they will bounce before they sink. They love watching the rows of little baby ducks following their mothers; they love talking to the geese and munching on picnics under the maple trees, which here are lush. And omnipresent. We live embraced, we live loved, by nature.

And in winter, there are homemade rinks on the river ice, far as the eye can see going east and west, where kids of all ages play ice hockey, people of all ages drag their huts out to engage in ice fishing, and figure skaters do their toe jumps, their flips, their Salchows, their Lutzes, their triple Axels, sometimes right in front of people's living room windows, a private show for the lucky. And the air, all the way from the Arctic Ocean — two thousand kilometres of land uninterrupted by development — fills your lungs to the point of bursting so that the very act of breathing is actually a singing, singing to the land that gave you this gift. And your spirit floats...

But the river has its moods; it has its tempers. It has been known, for instance, to overflow its banks come spring thaw, when the winter has produced more snow than expected. Wychwood has been flooded on many occasions, houses have been damaged, and some people have been left homeless. It is only a matter of time before the floods go haywire and wipe out entire cities and kill thousands. And if the rivers and the lakes don't do that, then the forest fires will. We here in Wychwood live a mere fifteen-minute drive, going inland, from the entrance to one of the most beautiful national parks in Canada. A maple forest of most extraordinary beauty, with hiking and bicycle and ski trails winding through it, Gatineau Park is a national treasure. But when will it burst into flame because of extreme heat precipitated by climate change, leaving us nothing but charred remains?

I sit on my Adirondack chair in the heat of

the summer and watch my grandchildren gambolling in the waters of the winding, murmuring river. They'll be fine, I think. But will *their* children? The Ottawa River is already radioactive. It's already sick.

My grandchildren are eight and ten. I just turned seventy. For the sake of future generations, will we let the patriarchal God of monotheism continue destroying the planet with his straight line of aggression? Or will we let his wife, the Mother Earth of Indigenous pantheism, preserve it for her children, for our grandchildren and great-grandchildren, with her womb, with her great, never-ending circle?

WHEN MY LITTLE BROTHER, René, went away — and went away is what happened, for, to me, he did not die, and he most certainly did not go to hell — I went to the hospital every day for the last two weeks of his life, for he faded very slowly, day by day. Movement by movement, faculty by faculty, organ by organ, nerve by nerve, they all stopped functioning until all that was left moving was his heart. And I'd sleep there in his hospital room, sometimes under his bed — yes, on the hard, cold linoleum with no sheets, no blanket — and some-times right there on the bed beside him, my arms around him, his sheets entangled around me. And I'd drift off. And in that space between sleep and awakeness, the dreams would drift in and out of me as if the current of a river was passing through me, my bloodstream mixed in with its liquid.

We are paddling in a sleek blue canoe, my younger brother and I, the way we used to as children, I at the stern, he at the bow. And we are paddling and paddling through the heart of the night, this thick mist swirling around us. We are heading for an island in the distance. The only sound is the rippling of water stirred by paddles. Until, as we approach the shroud-enveloped island, we hear singing, steady, pentatonic, almost like a Gregorian chant. Men and women — and children, too — are singing. And they are accompanied by the beating of a drum, its rhythm as regular as the beating of a human heart.

It is the dead who are singing. It is our ances-tors going back generation after generation, for we, as the mist gives way, recognize them one after another after another — our four sisters and one brother who left us as children, our father's parents, our mother's parents, our father's grandparents, our mother's grandparents, our laughing aunt Margaret, our elegant aunt Adele, our movie-star-handsome uncle William, cousins, cousins, and yet more cousins, friends, friends, and yet more friends. And they are dancing. We can see them clearly now, if still at a distance. They are dancing in a slow and rhythmic circle.

We arrive at the shore of the island. We beach the canoe. My brother disembarks, and I am about to follow him, for I want, with all my heart, to go with him. Without speaking, he turns to face me and, with one hand raised, motions me to stop. So I sit there frozen. With the hint of a smile curling his lip, he pushes the boat from the shore, this sandy bar, and it begins drifting away. My heart cries out but makes no noise. I drift off, farther and farther and farther and farther, he still standing on the shore, gently waving, gently smiling. And he is looking at me, the last I will see of the glimmer in his eyes.

As he turns to join the ancestors in their dance of life everlasting, the swirling fog swallows his figure. And I am left alone inside that boat, drifting and drifting and drifting. And weeping and weeping and weeping, the silence now total, except for the rippling of water as coaxed by the movement of a swirling paddle. Away up overhead, an eagle glides a graceful curve and guides me into the breaking light of day. And home.

I wake up in my brother's bed on the fifth floor at the Toronto Western Hospital, with my face, and the pillow that we share, drenched with tears. At eighteen days short of thirty-six, my younger brother, the achingly beautiful modern dancer René Highway, is still alive, if only barely. But I know, inside my heart, inside my blood, that he is on his way to the island of the dead and will be gone within two weeks.

I am nowhere near as beautiful as my younger brother, may he rest in peace. But then who could be? He passed into the spirit world at thirty-five, when I was thirty-eight, of AIDS. I don't miss him. He lives still with me every moment of my life. He brings me joy. I have, after all, his fulsome lips, I have his voice, I have his body. Yes, I once had the body of a ballet dancer; we all did — seven surviving children and two parents. Joe Highway, athlete supreme, passed on to us most excellent genes. My younger brother's last words to me before he slid into unconsciousness for his last two weeks on Earth were: "Don't mourn me, be joyful." So my job is to be joyful, not for one person, not for myself, but for two people: him and me. Which is why you will always see me having twice as good a time as everyone in any given room, at any given time. I have no time for tears; I am too busy being joyful.

A BRIEF GUIDE TO CREE

THE SOFT "G" AS IN "GEM" exists not in Cree. Only the hard "g" as in "gone" does. With exceptions, words with two or more syllables generally put the stress on the second. For newcomers to the language, the double consonant is hard to pronounce. The most common instance is when the "n" is followed by the "g" as in "n'gagee-waan" ("I will go home"). Another is when the "n" is followed by the "t" as in "n'taythee-tam" ("he/she wants it"). Much less common is the triple consonant as when the "k" is followed by the "s" is followed by the "ch" as in "k's'chees-naanis" ("brother" in the context liturgical) or "k's'kiman" ("file," the tool for woodwork). And rare is the quadruple consonant as in "poost-ska" ("put on" in the imperative as in "put on the shirt").

Then there's the double vowel, "ao," that is so common it amounts to a vowel on its own; "naapao" ("man"), "iskwao" ("woman"), and "kinoosao" ("fish") are sterling examples. If you pronounce the "a" of "ao" as in "day" and the "o" as in "owe" and squish them together, you will get the desired "ay-oh" where the separation of the syllables is rendered inaudible.

Now, because, as with all Indigenous languages in all three Americas, Cree was unwritten before the emergence of the present generation of Native writers, a happy by-product is the fact that a writer such as me has the licence to spell words the way they sound. Thus the following...

There are two kinds of "a" in Cree, the short and the long. A good illustration of both appears in the word for "snowshoes" which is "asaa-mak." In such cases, I take the liberty of spelling the first syllable, which is clipped, with a single "a," while the second, which is elongated, I spell with a double "a" as shown in the word just spelled: asaa-mak. An instance in English would be "canal," which, rightly speaking, should be spelled "canaal." For those of us whose mother tongue is not English, this would have been of immense help throughout those years we were learning the language, a task that, for us, was all but impossible. Which is not to say that the linguistic peregrination encountered in this book is not filled with pitfalls that stem from the crux that anchors our language: the long and the short "a." Examples are "saagay-higan" and "sagay-higan" (with the hard "g" in both cases), which sound (and look) quite similar but have two meanings, "lake" in the former and "nail" (as in carpentry) in the latter. Another example: "pasoo," which means "smell" in the imperative as in "smell this cheese" and "paasoo," which means "he/she is dry" (in the sense of humidity as opposed to abstinence from alcohol).

One last point that bears explaining is the syllable "ow." Examples are "oogow" ("pickerel"), "paag'wow" ("it is shallow" in the sense of water), and "nipow" ("sleep"). Without exception are they pronounced as in "cow," not as in "low."

A footnote on spelling: frequently consisting of five to eight syllables and sometimes more, Cree words are long and therefore difficult for non-Cree speakers to read, let alone pronounce. Example: niweecheewaaganak ("my friends"). To facilitate the process, I often take the liberty of dividing such words with a hyphen after every two syllables as in "niwee-cheewaa-ganak." You see? Easier to read, easier to pronounce.

READING LIST

I list here only a selection of the sources I drew upon in this work and that I recommend readers explore for their edification and enjoyment. In some cases, the works are available in multiple languages, translations, and formats, but I list only one as a place to begin.

Alighieri, Dante. *The Divine Comedy.* Translated by Henry Wadsworth Longfellow. New York: Houghton Mifflin, 1904.

The Bible: Authorized King James Version. Oxford World's Classics. Edited by Robert Carroll and Stephen Prickett. Oxford: Oxford University Press, 2008.

Deloria, Vine, Jr. *God Is Red: A Native View of Religion.* New York: Grosset & Dunlap, 1973.

Duchartre, Pierre Louis. *The Italian Comedy.* Translated by Randolph T. Weaver. New York: Dover Books, 1966.

Dyer, George J. *Limbo: the Unsettled Question.* New York: Sheed & Ward, 1964.

Erdoes, Richard, and Alfonso Ortiz. *American Indian Trickster Tales.* London: Penguin Books, 1999.

Frazer, James George. *The Golden Bough: A Study in Magic and Religion*. New York: The Macmillan Company, 1923.

Freud, Sigmund. *Totem and Taboo*. New York: Modern Library, 1938.

Frye, Northrop. *Words with Power: Being a Second Study of "The Bible and Literature."* Edited by Michael Dolzani. Toronto: University of Toronto Press, 2008.

Gibbon, Edward. *History of the Decline and Fall of the Roman Empire*. Edited by Hans-Friedrich Mueller. New York: Modern Library, 2003.

Graves, Robert. *The Greek Myths*. London: Penguin Books, 1992.

Homer. *The Odyssey*. Translated by Alexander Pope. Edited by Maynard Mack. London: Methuen, 1967.

Joyce, James. *Ulysses*. Paris: Shakespeare & Company, 1922.

Jung, C. G. *Memories, Dreams, Reflections*. Edited by Aniela Jaffé. Translated by Richard and Clara Winston. New York: Vintage Books, 1998.

Jung, Carl G., M.- L. von Franz, Joseph Henderson, Jolande Jacobi, and Aniela Jaffé. *Man and His Symbols*. Edited by Carl Jung and M.- L. von Franz. New York: Anchor Press, 1964.

Le Goff, Jacques. *The Birth of Purgatory*. Translated by Arthur Goldhammer. Chicago: University of Chicago Press, 1984.

McDannell, Colleen, and Bernhard Lang. *Heaven: A History*. New Haven, CT: Yale University Press, 1988.

McGaa, Ed. *Mother Earth Spirituality: Native American Paths to Healing Ourselves and Our World*. San Francisco: HarperCollins Publishing, 1990.

Milton, John. *Paradise Lost*. Norton Critical Edition. Edited by Gordon Teskey. New York: W. W. Norton & Company, 2004.

Neihardt, John G. *Black Elk Speaks*. Lincoln: University of Nebraska Press, 2004.

Oreglia, Giacomo. *The Commedia dell'Arte*. Translated by Lovett F. Edwards. London: Methuen, 1968.

Ovid. *Metamorphoses*. Translated by A. D. Melville. Oxford: Oxford University Press, 2008.

Pagels, Elaine. *The Origin of Satan*. New York: Random House, 1995.

———. *Why Religion? A Personal Story*. New York: HarperCollins Publishers, 2018.

Pagels, Heinz R. *The Cosmic Code: Quantum Physics as the Language of Nature*. New York: Simon & Schuster, 1982.

Panati, Charles. *Sacred Origins of Profound Things*. New York: Penguin Arkana, 1996.

Plato. *The Symposium*. Translated by Richard L. Hunter. Oxford: Oxford University Press, 2004.

Ray, Carl, and James R. Stevens. *Sacred Legends*. Ottawa: Penumbra Press, 1995.

Restany, Pierre. *Hundertwasser*. London: Parkstone Press, 2007.

Schumann, Robert. "Carnaval, Op. 9." In Robert Schumann's *Werke, Serie VII: Für Pianoforte zu zwei Händen*. Edited by Clara Schumann. Leipzig, Germany: Breitkopf & Härtel, 1879.

Shakespeare, William. *The Norton Shakespeare*. Third edition. Edited by Stephen Greenblatt, Walter Cohen, Suzanne Gossett, Jean E. Howard, Katharine Eisaman Maus, and Gordon McMullan. New York: W. W. Norton & Company, 2016.

Storm, Hyemeyohsts. *Seven Arrows*. New York: Ballantine Books, 1972.

· READING LIST ·

Turner, Alice K. *A History of Hell*. New York: Harcourt Brace, 1993.

Virgil. *The Aeneid*. Translated by John Dryden. New York: Heritage Press, 1944.

Yeats, William Butler. *The Collected Works of William Butler Yeats*. Edited by Richard J. Finneran. New York: Scribner, 1997.

ACKNOWLEDGEMENTS

THE AUTHOR THANKS THE FOLLOWING PEOPLE for help with this book: my publishing agent, Jackie Kaiser, Westwood Creative Artists; my theatrical agent, Kate Mensour; Greg Kelly, CBC *Ideas*; Philip Coulter, CBC *Ideas*; my life partner, Raymond Lalonde; my grandchildren, Marek and Milena Faucher; their mother, Alexie Lalonde-Steedman; their father, Louis-Jean Faucher (the last two for letting me use their children's names in this book); the most important teacher I have ever had in my life, the pianist William Aide and his wife, Heidi, both of whom gave me the strength that I needed to help me make my life the marvel that it is today; my copy editor, Stuart Ross, who gave this text the gentle touch that it needed to see the light of day; all the wonderful people at House of Anansi Press; and, most especially, my editor, Shirarose Wilensky, whose process was absolute magic — I was blown away. Lastly, I thank my parents and all the Elders to whom I owe my life, and who have told me many of these Trickster stories over the course of a lifetime.

(THE CBC MASSEY LECTURES SERIES)